COCKR P9-DHO-482

Cockrell Hill Public Library
4125 W. Clarendon Dr.
Dallas, TX 75211
(214) 330-9935

6th Edition

# How to Live – and Die – With

Please return your book/tape on time or call to renew:
Cockrell Hill Public Library, 4125 W. Clarendon
214-330-9935
There is a 24-hour book drop in the Police Station

**Gulf Publishing Company**
**Houston, Texas**

## 6th Edition

# How to Live – and Die – With

# TEXAS PROBATE

Wills, Trusts, and
Estate Planning in
Layman's Language

*Contains the latest information
on the federal income tax law
and state legislation*

## Charles A. Saunders, Editor
### In association with
### THE STATE BAR OF TEXAS

Sixth Edition

How to Live—and Die—With

# TEXAS PROBATE

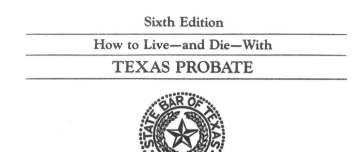

Copyright © 1968, 1974, 1978, 1983, 1988, 1990 by Gulf Publishing Company, Houston, Texas. All rights reserved. Printed in the United States of America. This book, or parts thereof, may not be reproduced in any form without permission of the publisher.

10  9  8  7  6  5  4

Gulf Publishing Company
Book Division
P.O. Box 2608 Houston, TX 77252-2608

**Library of Congress Cataloging-in-Publication Data**

How to live—and die—with Texas probate: wills, trusts, and estate planning in layman's language/ Charles A. Saunders, editor, in association with the State Bar of Texas.—6th ed.
  p.  cm.
"Contains the latest information on the federal income tax law and state legislation."
**ISBN 0-87201-922-5**
1. Estate planning—Texas. 2. Wills—Texas. 3. Probate law and practice—Texas. 4. Inheritance and transfer tax—Law and legislation—Texas. 5. Inheritance and transfer tax—Law and legislation—United States. I. Saunders, Charles A. II. State Bar of Texas.
KFT1344.Z9H68    1990                                89-78135
343.76405'3—dc20   [347.640353]                      CIP

# Contents

*tion of the Property. Provision for Common Accident or Successive Deaths. Powers for the Executor. Provision for Guardianship. Contingent Management Provision. Required Formalities. "Self-Proved" Will.*

*Discounted Treasury Bonds Accepted at Par for Estate Tax Payment. Application of the "Unlimited Throwback Rule." Community Property and Revocable Trusts.*

# Preface

The law of Probate—the law dealing with transmission of property from a decedent to his beneficiaries—is centuries old, yet little understood. Every adult citizen should understand the purpose of probate, the people it protects, and the advantages it offers; and with this understanding be motivated to plan his or her estate to achieve probate's highest purposes, protections, and advantages.

To make known to thoughtful Texans the basic concepts of probate and the considerable benefits of proper planning and use of probate, the Council of the Real Estate, Probate & Trust Law Section of the State Bar of Texas has undertaken publication of this book. With deep gratitude the Council acknowledges the work of some of the finest attorneys in the state of Texas in the preparation of this sixth edition:

| | |
|---|---|
| Lise E. Anderson | Dallas |
| Thomas D. Anderson | Houston |
| Arthur H. Bayern | San Antonio |
| John L. Bell, Jr. | Beaumont |
| Thomas E. Berry | Houston |
| Harvie Branscomb, Jr. | Corpus Christi |
| James E. Brill | Houston |
| W. Fred Cameron | Houston |
| Gordon R. Carpenter | Dallas |
| Harold A. Chamberlain | Houston |
| J. Chrys Dougherty | Austin |
| Joseph P. Hammond | El Paso |
| Allan Howeth | Fort Worth |
| H. David Hughes | Austin |

| Paul E. Martin | Houston |
| Lucian E. Morehead | Plainview |
| C. Stephen Saunders | Austin |
| Carroll B. Wheeler | Texarkana |
| Edward B. Winn | Dallas |
| Walter P. Zivley | Houston |

The Council also wishes to express sincere appreciation for significant contributions to previous editions by

Charles L. Cobb
Lawrence B. Gibbs
Robert Hobbs
Edwin P. Horner
Jack Gray Johnson
William I. Marschall
Dean Moorehead
Jack M. Vaughan
Thomas H. Wharton, Jr.

Every effort has been made to interpret in this book, fully and fairly, major facets of probate—to present the subject in a well balanced and readable form. The authors experienced difficulty in avoiding the use of technical expressions and in selecting terms with which the reader is familiar. This book is not intended to be a do-it-yourself substitute for carefully made estate plans and, on the contrary, is intended to point up the folly of homemade wills and amateur decisions about probate. General principles have been stated to provide an overall view of the subject. The reader with expertise will notice that certain exceptions to general rules have been omitted. The authors felt that the reader should have an understanding of general principles unencumbered by exceptions. Thus, the importance of personal consultation with the family lawyer proficient in the fields of estate planning and probate cannot be overemphasized.

To those native-born who have known the blessings of this great state all their lives, and to those who have displayed their good judgment in becoming Texas citizens by adoption, this book is dedicated.

*Charles A. Saunders, Editor*
Houston, Texas

6th Edition

# How to Live – and Die – With

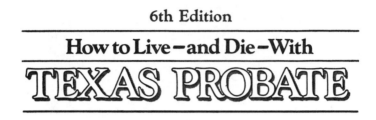

# 1

# What Is Community Property?

The ancient Goths were an aggressive tribe of northern Europe whose dominion had spread to most of western Europe by the sixth century. It is said that the women fought alongside their men and thus became entitled to an equal share of the spoils of war. The laws which encoded this tradition accompanied the Goths as they invaded first France and then Spain. The French version ultimately formed the basis for the property laws of Louisiana, and the Spanish version became engrained in the laws of Mexico and its colonies, including much of the area of the southwestern United States. By the time of the Louisiana Purchase, followed by Texas's independence from Mexico, equal division of marital property between husband and wife was well established from Louisiana westward. This eventually became the basic property law in eight states, including Texas. Other states where the community property system exists are Idaho, Arizona, California, Louisiana, New Mexico, Nevada, Washington, and, to a limited extent, Oklahoma. There are some variations in the laws of these eight states, and discussion will be confined to the law of Texas.

To determine what community property is, it is first necessary to consider what it is not. Property owned by a husband or wife before marriage is that person's *separate property*. Property received after marriage by gift or inheritance is separate property, as is a judgment for pain and suffering following an injury to either spouse. *Community property* is what is left. That is, community property in Texas is all property acquired by either spouse during marriage which is not separate property.

In case of doubt about the nature of a particular asset, it will be presumed to be community property and will be so judged in the absence of clear and convincing evidence establishing it as separate. A judgment for loss of earnings due to injury (in contrast to a recovery for pain and suffering) is treated as community.

The legal principles are simple enough, but their application can be extremely difficult, partly because the question of what is separate and what is community usually does not arise until the marriage is terminated by death or divorce. In the first case, one of the persons knowing essential facts is dead. In the second, the evidence of how and when certain assets were acquired may be tinged with bitterness and therefore unreliable. This is proved by hundreds of Texas court decisions in which courts have been called upon to determine which marital asset is community and which is separate.

### Record Keeping and Tracing

If the husband and wife have the foresight and the financial means to establish and maintain a reliable set of records, carefully segregating separate assets and channeling all cash receipts in the proper manner, there is little difficulty in determining the character of their assets when the marriage is dissolved. On the other hand, if records are poorly kept or if cash revenues have been indiscriminately mingled without regard to their source, the determination can become difficult, even impossible. Courts will make every effort to trace a questionable asset to its source, but if there is no evidence that the asset is the separate property of either spouse, it will be presumed to be community and so treated by the court. Tracing assets has long been a popular activity for accountants, lawyers and judges confronted with questions of this kind.

### Revenues from Separate Property

A large part of the trouble in distinguishing separate property from community property results from the assumption by many couples that revenue from a separate asset is itself separate. Unfortunately, for such persons the opposite is true unless they have entered into an agreement of the kind described in the following paragraph. Texas courts have long held that income from a separate asset is to be treated as community property. This includes rent from separate real estate; delay rentals from an oil and gas lease covering separately owned real estate; salaries, wages, and other earnings of both husband and wife; interest and cash dividends on separately owned securities; and profits from the sale of separately owned livestock. Without a written agreement, the only kinds of revenues considered to be the separate property of the spouse who owns the asset from which such revenues are derived are those which represent the return of capital, such as oil and gas royalties, a bonus received for making the lease, and stock dividends and splits

In 1980 an amendment to the Texas constitution was adopted which provides that a couple may agree, either prior to or during marriage, that the income or property arising from the separate property then owned by one of them, or which may thereafter be acquired, shall be the separate property of the owner. Such an agreement must be in writing and signed by both parties. The agreement is void if it is determined that the intent of the document is to defraud preexisting creditors. When the agreement involves real property, it must be acknowledged and recorded in the county in which the real property is located in order to serve as constructive notice to a good-faith purchaser for value or a creditor without actual notice.

That same constitutional amendment also provides that when one spouse makes a gift of property to the other spouse, it is presumed that the gift includes all the income or property which might arise from the gift, so that the spouse receiving the gift will own as his or her separate property not only the property itself but also whatever income is later produced by that property.

A profit from the sale of a separately owned asset is usually treated as the separate property of the spouse concerned. (The extent to which this may be taxed as a capital gain to both husband and wife under U.S. income tax laws is beyond the purpose of this chapter.)

## Partitioning the Community

Prior to 1948 it was not legally permissible for husband and wife to convert their community estate to separate property. In that year, however, a constitutional amendment removed the prohibition and enabled the 1949 legislature to prescribe a manner in which a husband and wife could voluntarily partition all or part of their community into separate property. A written instrument, signed by both parties, is all that is required now. Such a partition is not valid as to creditors or good faith purchasers without notice until the instrument is placed of record in the county where any real property is situated.

Community property may also be converted to separate property through a gift of such property from one spouse to the other as long as there exists the requisite donative intent and the gift is not made so as to defraud or injure creditors or other third parties.

As noticed later, one's community property may be disposed of by will, and if there is no will, it is inherited according to state law. A notable exception is found in the statutes permitting married people to enter into contracts with banks or other financial institutions that permit the surviving spouse to become the owner of the fund when the other spouse dies. An even more notable exception became law in November 1987, when the electorate adopted an amendment to the Texas Constitution permitting married persons to "agree in writing that all or part of their community property becomes the property of the surviving spouse on the death of a spouse." In other words, by contract, married persons are now in a position to convert community assets to something similar to the arrangement known in common-law states as "joint tenancy with the right of survivorship."

Care should be taken that such a contract is consistent with one's estate plan, of which a will is an essential part. To use the "agree(ment) in writing" as a substitute for a will may fail to dispose of one's entire estate, whereupon a relative or even a creditor may require that an administrator be appointed. The administrator must post a bond and seek court approval of all his actions—far more awkward than probating a will which names an independent executor. (The impact of estate and inheritance taxes may also produce some rude surprises.)

Texas law contains no provision for converting separate property to community property by a deed or other voluntary act of the parties. An attempt to do so would probably result in a tenancy-in-common. However, a "scrambling" of separate and community funds, if carried on long enough, would probably result in an eventual loss of the proof that an asset was originally separate and, as noted, in the absence of such proof, the asset will be presumed to be community.

The community estate of newcomers to Texas begins when their first earnings or other community receipts reach their hands. There is no automatic conversion into community property of assets previously acquired; real estate (land and buildings) in the former state, as well as personal property brought into this state, will remain the separate property of the owners if it was separate when acquired. But such an asset may lose its separate character through changes in form or from mingling community receipts with the separate asset, since the new resident's personal property is judged by Texas law without regard to the state where he was married or the fact that the asset may have originated in the other state.

Married persons who leave Texas do not thereby convert their community estate to separate property. Texas real estate, if community property at the time of the owners' removal, will remain so, and the determination whether it is community or separate is a question of Texas law. Even the courts of another state would apply Texas law if the question arose there. Property other than land follows the owner and loses some of its community attributes when the owners move to a non-community property state and become subject to the laws of their new residence. Normally the courts of the new state of residence will hold that property other than land is owned in equal undivided shares by the husband and wife.

Generally speaking, the community is dissolved by the death of one spouse. In the absence of a will, the survivor has the legal right to continue the management of the community, but this right is sharply diminished where the decedent has left a will and an executor has been appointed by the court.

Either spouse can dispose of all his property, separate or community, by a valid will. Indeed, it is not uncommon for the decedent to leave a will which undertakes to dispose of the survivor's share of the community estate as well as his own, perhaps substituting an interest in the decedent's separate estate for the community interest otherwise bequeathed. But the survivor is not bound to acquiesce in such an arrangement and may elect to take his or her community interest in lieu of taking under the will. Although this is sometimes referred to as "the widow's election," it is also available to surviving husbands.

In the absence of a will, the law specifies how all property of a deceased person shall be distributed. This subject is fully covered in subsequent chapters, in which it will be noticed that community property is inherited differently from separate property—another reason why every person who owns property should make a will.

## Management of the Community

Thus far we have discussed *property* rights of husband and wife, as outlined in our state constitution, statutes, and appellate court decisions. The discussion that follows is concerned with *management* rights as now set forth in the Texas Family Code.

For centuries the husband was the exclusive manager of the community including that portion derived from the wife's separate estate or from her personal earnings. A law enacted in 1968 virtually eliminated the husband's exclusive management and placed the wife on an equal footing. The law now says that each spouse shall have sole management and control of his or her personal earnings, the revenues from his or her separate property, the recoveries for personal injuries awarded to him or her, and the increase, mutations, and revenues of all property subject to his or her sole management and control. If community property subject to one spouse's control becomes mixed or combined with community property subject to the control of the other spouse, then such property is to be jointly managed and controlled by both spouses unless they agree otherwise. All other community property is subject to the joint management of the husband and wife.

Moreover, an asset held in the name of either spouse, or in his or her exclusive possession, is now presumed to be "subject to his or her sole management," and in the absence of contrary notice or fraud, a third person may safely deal with and receive good title from the spouse who has exclusive possession or in whose name the asset is registered. A new section of the insurance code extends this rule to insurance contracts, giving the spouse in whose name the contract is registered full authority to deal with it without the signature of the other spouse.

In case of a permanent separation of the parties, or if one disappears or is missing in action, or if one spouse abandons the other or becomes unable to manage his or her portion of the community, the other spouse may apply to the district court for permission to become the sole manager of the community. Provision is made for similar court relief where one spouse is frustrated in selling a homestead due to the incompetence, disappearance, abandonment, or separation of the other spouse; without such circumstances, the joinder of husband and wife is still required for the conveyance or encumbrance of the homestead.

The 1968 statutes were designed to place the wife on an equal footing with her husband in the management and disposition of community assets. The wife has long had the right to manage her separate estate. Now, it is clear, she also has the right to manage and dispose of any community assets registered in her name (e.g., a car, a stock certificate, a bank or savings account) or held in her exclusive possession or control. The husband has a corresponding right. If there is any doubt about the exclusiveness of possession or control by an individual spouse, a purchaser or creditor would be well-advised to obtain the signature of both spouses to the instrument evidencing the transfer or the security document.

## Summary

The community property system represents an equitable method of permitting the wife as well as the husband to participate in the fruits and profits to be derived from their joint efforts. All property acquired during marriage is presumed to be community property and will be treated so unless it can be shown to have its source in property owned before marriage or received later by gift or inheritance. Those having separate property and wishing to preserve its identity can do so by the maintenance of orderly records which carefully distinguish between separate principal and community income. Those persons who may wish to convert their community interests to separate estates may do so by signing a partition agreement; however, separate property may not be converted into community by agreement.

Although community and separate property interests are inherited differently where either spouse dies without a will, this effect can be avoided by executing a proper will.

# 2

# What Is My Probate Estate?

## The Word "Probate"

The word "probate" originally meant "to test and to prove." It came to mean the procedure of establishing before a court of proper jurisidiction that an instrument is the last will and testament of a deceased person.

In Texas, probate has come to include not only the determination by the probate court that an instrument is the last will and testament of the decedent, but the doing of all those things which the probate court has jurisdiction to do in settling estates.

Probate proceedings involve determining whether the deceased left a valid will; appointing and qualifying a personal representative for the estate; collecting the assets of the estate; preparing an inventory of the estate; preparing estate, inheritance, and income tax returns; establishing and paying claims and taxes; selling property to pay debts or to effect distribution of the estate; determining those who are entitled to receive the property of the estate and distributing their property to them; settling the accounts of the personal representative; discharging the personal representative and releasing the sureties on his bond; and closing the estate.

Under the Texas Constitution, the probate court is the county court established for each county. It is known in most counties as the county court, but in some counties it is known as the county court at law; and in a few larger counties as the probate court. Some counties have more than one court to handle probate cases.

## What Is a "Personal Representative"?

The personal representative of the estate of a deceased is the person authorized by the court to act for the estate. He is appointed by the court and qualifies by signing an oath and giving bond, if a bond is required. Banks and corporations with trust powers, as well as individuals, may act in this capacity. The personal representative is known as the executor if he is named in the will of the deceased, and as the administrator if he was not named in the will. The court will appoint as executor the person named in the will, unless some unusual reason compels a different appointment. The executor or administrator must make bond, unless the deceased has directed otherwise in his will or unless the executor is a bank with trust powers. The court may waive bond in certain cases.

The clerk of the court issues "letters testamentary" to an executor and "letters of administration" to an administrator after he has been appointed by the court, has filed his oath of office, and has made the bond required and approved by the court. "Letters testamentary" or "letters of administration" is a printed form certified by the court clerk that the holder is in charge of the estate and entitled to possession of the assets. Letters are evidence of authority to take charge of an estate and to act for it.

### What Is the "Estate"?

The estate of a person includes everything he owns. In this sense a person's estate is the aggregate of all his assets, riches, and fortune, and includes rights to receive income from property owned by another. One of the common uses of the word is to denote and describe, in a most general manner, the property and assets of a deceased person.

The "probate estate" of a deceased person is that part of his property and assets which the personal representative of his estate administers and which is subject to the applicable laws and terms of the will and control of the court. It does not include any property or assets of the deceased which do not pass into the hands of the personal representative. The probate estate of a deceased person exists from his death until all debts have been paid, the property has been distributed, and the personal representative has been discharged.

The probate estate is not to be confused with the "gross estate," as gross estate is defined for purposes of assessing the federal unified transfer tax. A deceased person may have owned or controlled property, or enjoyed income from property during his lifetime that is a part of his gross estate for tax purposes but is not a part of his probate estate. For example, the deceased during his lifetime may have disposed of certain assets which remain a part of his gross estate for tax purposes but not part of his probate estate. Common examples are:

1. Gifts made before the death of the donor. (Most gifts to any one person in any one year of a total value of $10,000 or less will not be a part of the taxable estate.)
2. Conveyances of property in which the grantor reserved income or control for his lifetime.
3. Trusts created by a person who reserved the right to revoke, alter, or amend the trust or to control the beneficial enjoyment of the property or to receive income during his lifetime.

Life insurance, payments under annuities and pension and retirement plans, bonds and property in joint tenancy, exempt property and property in trust may be included in the taxable estate, although it is not a part of the probate estate.

## *What Is Not Included in the Probate Estate?*

The "probate estate" does not include all of the property and assets owned by a deceased person during his lifetime. Even a person of modest means usually owns property said to be a part of his estate but which does not pass under his will and never becomes a part of his probate estate. Such property may include insurance, employee benefits, social security, bonds, property in joint tenancy, exempt property, and trust property.

## *Insurance*

Life insurance is payable on a person's death in the manner provided by the policy. It is usually made payable to a named beneficiary, and in the case of the prior or simultaneous death of the beneficiary, it is made payable to a contingent beneficiary. The insured is usually the owner of the policy, or the policy is part of the community estate of the insured and his wife. The proceeds of such a policy are not payable to the personal representative of the estate of the insured and do not become a part of his probate estate. However, the proceeds will be a part of the probate estate of the insured if they are made payable to his estate by the terms of the policy or if all named beneficiaries die before the proceeds become payable.

Moreover, jf there are no named and qualified primary or contingent beneficiaries, and if the insured owns the policy, the proceeds are payable to the personal representative of his estate. The proceeds are taxable if the decedent had an "incident of ownership" in the policy, or if it was payable to his personal representative.

### Annuities and Retirement Benefits

An annuity may be payable under what is known as an "annuity contract" or under an insurance policy with provisions for payment of benefits during the lifetime of the insured and, perhaps, thereafter. An individual may be the beneficiary of an annuity created by a contract purchased by him or purchased by another for him. He may be an employee of a corporation which had a pension plan or profit-sharing plan under which he and his spouse or dependents or some of them are entitled to payments. He or his employer may have created an Individual Retirement Account (IRA), a Keogh Plan, or other "simplified" pension plan. Any amounts payable after the death of the beneficiary will be payable according to the terms of the annuity contract, insurance policy, or pension plan. In most cases the amounts payable after the death of the beneficiary will not become a part of his probate estate.

### Social Security and Government Pensions

Social Security benefits and pensions payable under federal or state law do not become a part of the probate estate. These amounts may or may not be taxable. However, any amounts payable prior to the death of a beneficiary are payable to the personal representative of his estate as part of the probate estate.

### Bonds

United States Savings Bonds may be made payable to the deceased as owner or co-owner, or to a beneficiary named by the decedent. If the co-owner or named beneficiary survives the deceased, the survivor is the absolute owner of the bonds. They do not become a part of the decedent's probate estate, although they may be included, in whole or in part, in his gross estate for tax purposes. The United States Supreme Court has held that bonds purchased by Texans with community funds are not subject to the community property laws of Texas, and that federal law and Treasury regulations prevail over state law. Of course, these bonds will be a part of the probate estate of the surviving co-owner or named beneficiary if he still owns them at the time of his death and has not caused them to be reissued to himself as a co-owner or to a named beneficiary.

## Property in Joint Tenancy with Right of Survivorship

Many stocks, bonds, bank and savings and loan accounts, and other property are held by the deceased and another in joint tenancy with right of survivorship. It is not a part of the probate estate of the deceased. It passes to the surviving joint tenant upon the death of the deceased by operation of law and the contract made when the joint tenancy was created.

There is no right of survivorship unless it is so provided in precise language in a valid written instrument that is executed in compliance with Texas statutes.

Joint tenancy with right of survivorship is commonly used in other states, but under the Texas community property system the husband and wife each own an undivided half interest in their community property, and the need for joint tenancy is not the same as in other states.

Much litigation and uncertainty has resulted from attempts by spouses to convert their community property into joint tenancy with right of survivorship, and from arrangements that, perhaps unintentionally, created a right of survivorship. Amendments to our state constitution and statutes were intended to remove this uncertainty, but litigation and questions still arise.

A 1989 statute sets out requirements for conversion of community property to joint tenancy with right of survivorship. Some of these requirements are new and may make the conversion less attractive.

## Exempt Property

The widow, minor children, and unmarried daughters remaining with the family of a deceased person are entitled to that property of the estate which is exempt from execution or forced sale by the constitution and laws of the state. This includes the homestead, furnishings of the home, two vehicles, tools and equipment of trade or profession, implements of farming or ranching, a certain number of livestock, and some other items all within certain monetary limits. The court will set this property apart for their benefit immediately after the inventory, appraisement, and list of claims filed by the personal representative have been approved.

In case all or any of the specific articles exempt from execution or forced sale are not among the effects of the deceased, the court will make a reasonable allowance in lieu thereof. These items do not become a part of the probate estate and, with certain exceptions, are not subject to payment of debts of the deceased, but they are a part of his gross estate for tax purposes.

## Trust Property

Property conveyed by an individual to a trustee to be administered in trust and distributed after the individual's death usually is not a part of the probate estate. A person has a right to convey his property to a trustee to be held and administered in trust, with the income and property of the trust estate to be used and distributed as provided in the instrument. The grantor may make himself the trustee; he may reserve the right to alter, and amend, or revoke the trust during lifetime; he may make himself the beneficiary of the trust. The property of a trust of this kind generally would not be subject to administration by the personal representative and would not be a part of his probate estate, unless the trust terminated or was revoked by the grantor prior to death. In some cases the property of the trust would be subject to the payment of the decedent's debts. We have noted that in many cases the trust estate may be a part of the gross estate for tax purposes.

If the deceased was the trustee or beneficiary of a trust created by some other person, or if he was entitled to receive income from or use of property, these rights terminate upon death. The property in which he has these rights will not be part of the probate estate, except income payable to him or possibly other vested rights he had in the property at the time of his death, or unless he had what is known as a general power of appointment in property of the trust.

## Community Property

The interest of a decedent in community property passes to his spouse without administration if there is no will and if the decedent had no descendent. There is no probate estate in this case.

If the decedent had no will but did have children, the interest of both spouses in the community estate will be a probate estate administered by the surviving spouse as community administrator if she desires to qualify as such, or perhaps as community survivor if there are community debts and if she does not seek court appointment.

Where the decedent left a will that names an executor, the probate estate will include and the executor will administer the separate property of the deceased and also all of the interest of both spouses in community property, except the part that was legally under the sole management of the surviving spouse during the marriage.

The surviving spouse may by written instrument waive any right to exercise powers as community survivor, and in this event the entire community estate becomes a part of the probate estate of the decedent, and its executor or administrator is authorized to administer it. Contracts made by both spouses during the marriage or wills that require the surviving spouse to release her community share under the will may accomplish the same result.

## Withdrawing the Estate from Court

Persons entitled to the estate of the deceased may withdraw the estate from administration and take possession of it, provided they furnish a bond approved by the court for an amount equal to at least double the gross appraised value of the estate. The persons executing the bond agree to become responsible for all debts of the estate. Any person entitled to any portion of an estate withdrawn from further administration may cause a partition and distribution to be made among the persons entitled to it.

Certain "small" estates may not be subject to administration and other "small" estates may be withdrawn from administration.

### Summary

Not everything a person owns or considers his property will become a part of his probate estate. Large parts of the estate often go to beneficiaries outside the will. Care, then, should be taken to make certain that a sufficient amount of property (probate estate) will pass under the will to pay estate debts, take care of legacies, and accomplish the purposes intended by the will. Moreover, property may be a part of the gross estate of a decedent for federal tax purposes regardless of whether it is a part of his probate estate.

# 3

# When Is My Estate Valued And Why?

An estate is valued on several occasions and may be valued for several reasons. An initial reason is to obtain facts upon which to plan the most efficient and economical transfer of the estate to the persons who are to receive it after the death of the owner. The planning should be done during the lifetime of the owner of the estate. Taxes and expenses may be minimized to the extent permitted by law. The transfer may then be carried out according to the owner's wishes.

Therefore, the most important valuations of an estate are made during the owner's lifetime, when the owner can determine the disposition of the estate and can revise the plan as values or circumstances change. This is true whether the estate is large or small. The estates of both spouses should be valued in this planning stage. The owners can, by making these valuations, determine whether the estates consist of the desired kinds of properties and how far these properties will go in carrying out the desired intentions, whether the intentions are to protect a spouse, furnish an education for children, or for other purposes. These valuations afford opportunities for tax planning, as well as helping to determine the desirability of property exchange between spouses, equalizing their respective estates, or making lifetime gifts.

The owner, while living, has a free choice to decide how the transfer of the estate will be made. The owner may choose whether the order of descent and distribution of the estate will be determined by law, by the owner through transfer before death, in a will, or by other procedures that are available but can be used only if the owner elects to use them. Only by knowing values and purposes can the most efficient and economical transfer of properties be planned and achieved. These elections are made by every person, knowingly or unknowingly, when the individual makes a will, delays making a will, or simply decides not to make a will.

Valuations of an estate after the death of the owner are important under state and federal laws. The first valuation after death should include the probate and nonprobate estate subject to federal estate tax. Determination then can be made whether the federal estate tax laws apply. If they do, occasions for use of valuations of an estate are provided by the tax laws. The Texas Probate Code provides several procedures relating to the probate estate, and which procedure may apply is determined from a valuation of the probate estate. These valuations are determined as of the date of death of the decedent.

### Valuation for Special Probate Purposes

The Texas Probate Code provides for special handling of small estates. If the valuation made after death shows that the value of the assets of the estate (over and above the homestead and certain property protected by law as exempt from claims of creditors) does not exceed $50,000, then all of the probate estate can be delivered to the persons entitled to receive it. The delivery of the estate can be made upon approval by the county judge of an affidavit filed with the county clerk of the proper county as defined in the Code. This procedure can be followed when 30 days have elapsed after the death of the decedent if no petition has been filed for the appointment of an executor or administrator, and if no other court proceedings are necessary.

The Texas Probate Code also makes provision for the protection of a surviving spouse and minor children left without separate property or property in their own right adequate for their maintenance. The Code provides for a family allowance to be set in an amount sufficient for the maintenance of a surviving spouse and minor children for one year from the decedent's death. If the value of this allowance, together with the homestead and exempt property, exceeds the value of the whole estate, then the probate court, after payment of expenses of last illness and funeral, can order the properties distributed without further action.

The Texas Probate Code additionally provides that the homestead and other property exempt from claims of creditors shall be set apart for the use and benefit of the surviving spouse, minor children, and unmarried children remaining with the family. Where such items are not a part of the estate, a reasonable allowance from other property may be paid to the surviving spouse and children. The allowance in lieu of a homestead cannot exceed $10,000, and the allowance in lieu of other exempt property cannot exceed $1,000.

### Inventory Valuation

In the event there is an administration of an estate, either by an executor, an administrator, an independent executor, or a community administrator, the Probate Code specifies that an inventory of the estate must be filed in the probate court granting the administration by the appointed personal representative within 90 days from the time of appointment, although an extension of time to file the inventory may be granted by the court. An appraisement, or valuation of the fair market value, of each article of property must be included with the inventory. This valuation may be made by the personal representative from sources of his own selection, and he may seek assistance of appraisers. Upon application to the probate court by any person interested in the estate, including the personal representative, the court will appoint disinterested persons to appraise the property of the estate. The setting aside of the homestead and exempt property (or the allowances in lieu of the exempt property) and the allowances for family maintenance can then be determined. The inventory and appraisement also indicate to any creditors the extent of the estate for the payment of their claims.

The inventory and valuation furnish the basis from which the executor or administrator must account to the beneficiaries for the proper management of the estate, the payment of claims, and the delivery of the proper share to the persons so entitled. The inventory and appraisement must be corrected and supplemented if there are any omissions of properties, or if additional properties are discovered. Any interested person, including any beneficiaries or creditors, may bring such errors to the attention of the court for correction.

The inventory and appraisement also serve as a basis for the procedure of withdrawing an estate from administration, once administration has been granted by the probate court. They further give a basis for the amount of a bond required to secure the payment of creditors following the withdrawal from administration.

Finally, the inventory and appraisement provide the basis for the accounting to minors of their share of a community estate. This occurs when a surviving spouse administers community property (where there is no will) for a year without having guardians appointed for the minors during such time.

## *Valuation for Tax Purposes*

Regardless of any appraisement made during the course of proceedings under the Probate Code, there must be a valuation made of estates, whether large or small, for tax purposes. There is a practical, as well as a legal, necessity to demonstrate either that no taxes are due or that taxes due have been paid. This valuation is made and tax procedures complied with to enable timely payment of any taxes due and the distribution of the estate to the beneficiaries free of any tax lien.

A tax return may be required to be filed with Internal Revenue Service for federal estate tax purposes within nine months after the death of the decedent, depending upon the value of the estate. If death occurs during or after 1987 a return must be filed if the gross estate (before any allowances for debts, expenses, or other permitted deductions) is in excess of $600,000. A return may be required if the gross estate is less than $600,000 if the decedent claimed a specific exemption from federal gift taxes on gifts of property after September 8, 1976, or made taxable gifts after December 31, 1976.

The Tax Reform Act of 1986 reenacted a generation-skipping transfer tax which applies generally, with some exceptions, to direct transfers or transfers through the use of trusts where the beneficiaries are more than one generation below the generation of the transferor. An exemption of $1,000,000 is allowed each transferor, and a special $2,000,000 exemption per grandchild is allowed for direct transfers to, or under certain limitations in trust for, grandchildren if made before 1990. Death of a transferor or a transfer from a decedent under a will may be the occasion for the imposition of this tax. Valuations of property for any generation-skipping transfer tax to which the estate is subject may be the valuations used for estate tax purposes, and the generation-skipping transfer tax return is required to be filed with the estate tax return.

Texas law does not require a return to be filed for Texas inheritance tax purposes unless a federal estate tax return must be filed and the decedent was a resident of Texas or was a nonresident or an alien owning property taxable in Texas. A form furnished by the Texas comptroller of public accounts together with a copy of the federal estate tax return and any federal generation-skipping transfer tax return is to be filed with the comptroller within nine months after the decedent's death.

A certificate may be obtained from the Texas comptroller of public accounts if no Texas inheritance tax is due or all taxes due have been paid. Similar certificates may be issued by the Internal Revenue Service. These certificates may be filed in any probate proceedings, or if none, in any county where land belonging to the decedent is located.

Such tax returns present additional occasions to use valuations of an estate after death, and they provide for an election to be made as to whether the tax determination shall be made on the value of the estate on the date of the decedent's death or as of six months after the decedent's death.

### Value Six Months After Death

Using values as of six months after death is commonly referred to as using the "alternate valuation date." Under federal and Texas tax laws the alternate valuation date can be elected by the executor, administrator, or a representative of the estate. The purpose of this provision, born of the depression days of the 1930s, is to provide tax relief where there has been a decline in the values of an estate within six months after the decedent's death.

The election can be made only if the value of the gross estate on the alternate valuation date is less than the value of the gross estate on the date of death, and also results in less estate tax being paid than the estate tax that would be paid if based upon valuations at date of death. The alternate valuation date, if elected, is also the date of valuation in determining any generation-skipping transfer tax to which the estate may be subject, and the election must also decrease the sum total of any generation-skipping transfer tax and estate tax for the election to be effective. The alternate valuation date may be elected on an estate tax return that is filed with the Internal Revenue Service. Although extensions of time to file the federal estate tax return have been granted, the election must be on a return filed within one year after the original due date of the return.

Although the filing of a federal estate tax return may be required based on date of death values, determination of tax to be paid is made on alternate valuation date valuations, if the election is properly made. The election once made is irrevocable. If the election is made, all of the property in the estate must be valued as of the alternate date rather than the date of death (subject to a few special rules). However, if the alternate valuation date is used then any property distributed, sold, exchanged or otherwise disposed of within six months after the decedent's death is valued at the value on the date of distribution or disposition. The value of any interest that is affected by mere lapse of time, such as the paying out of annuity or the expiration of a patent, is not entitled to be revalued where the revaluation reflects only the passage of time.

The election may affect not only the estate tax and generation-skipping transfer tax, but also may affect income taxes of the surviving spouse or other beneficiaries of the decedent's estate. Properties acquired from a decedent generally take as a new basis for tax purposes the value at date of decedent's death, or, if elected, the alternate valuation date, unless a permitted special-use valuation method has been elected. The one half interest of the surviving spouse in community property likewise takes the new basis. The new basis may either step up or step down valuations of these properties for tax purposes with certain specified exceptions. The election will determine whether the valuation at date of death or on alternate valuation date will be the basis in determining federal income taxes upon a later sale or disposition of property received by the surviving spouse or other beneficiaries from the decedent's estate, as well as upon the later sale or disposition by the surviving spouse of his or her interest in community property.

One important exception to the stepped-up basis rule, among others, applies to property received by the decedent by gift within the one-year period before the decedent's death. If the donor of the property to the decedent (or donor's spouse) reacquires the property from the decedent's estate, the basis of the property in the hands of the donor or donor's spouse will be the same basis that the decedent had before his death, although the property had a higher value at decedent's death (or on alternate valuation date) and was subject to estate tax at a higher valuation. This exception prevents a donor from obtaining a stepped up basis in property given to a decedent within the short period prior to the decedent's death to minimize donor's income taxes on a subsequent sale by the donor (or his spouse) after reacquiring the property from the decedent's estate. The exception also applies when the donor (or donor's spouse) acquires the proceeds of a sale of such property made by the estate of the decedent.

## Special-Use Valuations

The Tax Reform Act of 1976 introduced concepts of special-use valuations for relief to farmers and owners of closely held businesses and, while these provisions are still in effect, the Economic Recovery Tax Act of 1981 (ERTA) made important changes applying to estates of persons dying after 1981.

If properly elected by the personal representative of the estate, and an agreement is signed by all persons having an interest in or considered to take from the decedent an interest in the subject property, qualified real estate (which is included in decedent's gross estate and used for farming purposes or in a closely held trade or business) may be valued for estate tax purposes on date of death, or, if elected, on the alternate valuation date, on the basis of its value for its actual use instead of the fair market value for its highest or best use. For example, a farm approached by urban expansion might have a higher market value for commercial development than for continued farming. The reduction in gross estate values by such election, however, cannot exceed in the aggregate $750,000 where decedent's death occurred in 1983 or thereafter.

For the election to apply after 1981, in addition to other requirements, the real property must have been used by the decedent or his family as a farm or in a trade or business; have been so used for at least five out of eight years prior to decedent's death, disability, or retirement with material participation by decedent or his family during such years (or prior years under certain circumstances); pass from the decedent to defined members of the family; have a value at least equal to 25% of the adjusted gross estate; and the value of the real property and personal property used in farming or in the trade or business must have a value equal to at least 50% of decedent's adjusted gross estate. The valuations used for the 25% and 50% tests are values of the highest and best use, rather than the actual use. Computations of the gross estate for these tests include gifts made by the decedent within three years prior to decedent's death. The inclusion of these gifts in the gross estate prevents deathbed gifts by the decedent of other property to qualify the farm or trade or business real property for the special-use valuations. A farm for this purpose includes, among other things, ranches, nurseries, orchards, and, subject to other special rules, woodlands. The tax law provides a formula for determining the actual value of farms using cash rental basis of comparable land, or if none, net share rental of comparable land, and other factors. Other methods may, however, be used for determining the actual value of the real estate used in farming or in the trade or business.

The benefit of these special-use valuations may depend on facts in existence years prior to the decedent's death, with valuations of property and estates necessary well in advance of valuations traditionally considered necessary only after the death of the decedent.

The estate tax benefits realized by these special-use valuations may be recaptured by a tax imposed upon the recipients of the property from the decedent if within 10 years after the decedent's death the qualified property is transferred out of the defined family, or the property ceases to be used (with some exceptions) for the purpose for which the special-use valuation was intended.

## Other Valuations

This chapter has discussed primarily when and why valuations of an estate are made, whether before or after a decedent's death. However, ERTA and other recent laws suggest that valuations of estates of a surviving spouse or of other beneficiaries of the decedent's estate should parallel valuations of the decedent's estate. ERTA provided substantial increases in the unified credit in computation of federal estate taxes. The equivalent exemption was increased from $175,000 in the case of a decedent whose death occurred in 1981 to $600,000 where death occurs in 1987 or thereafter. An unlimited marital deduction is provided under federal estate and gift tax laws for interspousal gifts and bequests after 1981. The increase in equivalent exemption and the unlimited marital deduction are two of the bases for this suggestion.

In the case of a husband and wife, using the unified credit in each estate may achieve non-taxable transfers of both estates depending on the total valuation of each estate. Any part of the estate transferred to a surviving spouse defers estate tax attributable to such transfer until the death of the surviving spouse. The estate of the surviving spouse, valued at the date of death or on alternate valuation date, is entitled to the benefit of only the one equivalent exemption and is taxed at rates effective upon the death of the surviving spouse. The estate of the surviving spouse includes that part transferred from the first estate. Since estate tax rates are graduated upward, the resulting tax may be greater than the total of lesser taxes assessed separately on the two estates if other dispositions of property had been made in the first estate. The valuation of the estate of each spouse, and the projected valuation of the estate of the surviving spouse, should therefore be considered in determining transfers between spouses, either during their lives or by reason of death.

ERTA also introduced another occasion for comparing valuations of the estates of the husband and wife. This comparison, however, is made by the personal representative of the estate of the spouse whose death occurs first and may be made nine months after such death occurs, or up until fifteen months after such death if the filing of the estate tax return has been properly extended until such time. ERTA allows a "qualified terminable interest property" (QTIP) trust to be created providing income to the surviving spouse for life but upon death of the surviving spouse passing the trust estate to children or other beneficiaries designated by the creator of the trust. The personal representative may be authorized to elect on the timely filed federal estate tax return the extent to which the trust will qualify for a marital deduction. This election results in federal estate taxes on the first estate to the extent the marital deduction is deferred to the estate of the surviving spouse; or the election may result, in effect, in allocating the tax between the two estates. This election presents an opportunity to the personal representative to consider, among other factors, tax effects based on actual valuations of the two estates determined after the death of the first spouse. These valuations may have been difficult to determine accurately prior to such time. The election also gives flexibility in determining ultimate tax liabilities by taking into account the increased amounts of the equivalent exemption from federal estate tax effective after 1981.

Federal tax laws, as well as property laws of most states, including Texas, permit a beneficiary of an estate (including a surviving spouse) to refuse to accept all or any part of a bequest or inheritance from a decedent by properly executing and properly filing a written disclaimer within nine months after the death of the decedent. The effect is to transfer the bequest or inheritance that is disclaimed to other persons who would have been the beneficiaries of such bequest or inheritance had the person disclaiming been deceased on the death of the decedent. This procedure, in effect, permits a tax-free transfer by the disclaiming beneficiary to another, for example, from a surviving spouse to children, or children to grandchildren. The purpose may be to shift income from the disclaimed property from one to another for resulting income tax savings, or to minimize the estate of the disclaiming beneficiary for resulting estate tax savings. Valuation of estates of the first beneficiaries of the decedent, as well as the estates of persons who might take assets of the decedent's estate as a result of a disclaimer, may be looked to both for income tax and estate tax consequences; and these valuations may be made within the nine months after the death of the decedent.

## Summary

Valuation, as discussed in this chapter, whether for planning, fixing family allowances, determining taxes due or not due, or using the alternate valuation date, is the determination of the market value of property on the proper dates except where special-use valuations are permitted. Valuations may be determined by a variety of methods, depending on the type of property involved, and for tax purposes by application of special tax rules. By proper valuations at the proper times, the desires of the decedent with the maximum benefits to the decedent's beneficiaries can be planned and achieved.

# 4

# The Debts I Have
# Created—How Paid

In the course of a lifetime every person creates debts. The size and nature of these obligations vary with individual and family situations. It is not surprising that the biggest debts usually are created by the wealthiest people because they have the assets, collateral, and credit rating to support larger borrowings. Unfortunately, many families of average means obligate themselves beyond their abilities to pay, causing financial problems during lifetime and most certainly after death. The biggest obligation is usually the mortgage on the home. In addition there may be innumerable time payments for cars, appliances, and other items. In any event, these obligations may become a factor to deal with in the administration of an estate.

Take the case of a husband and wife with minor children. If the husband lives to retirement, the mortgage on the home will normally be paid off, along with many other items purchased on credit. But what if the husband dies unexpectedly at an earlier age? He leaves the wife to support the minor children and pay the financial obligations. Further, the main source of income—the husband's earning capacity—is gone. This situation can create quite a hardship on the surviving family members. Therefore, it is the wise man who provides protection for his family in the event of his death.

*Provisions in the Will*

Most wills provide for an independent executor of the estate to pay debts, taxes, and the cost of administration. Whether or not the will so provides, the executor is under a general duty to pay obligations of the decedent's estate. Community debts—those created during marriage—are primarily payable out of the total community shares upon the death of either. A direction by the testator in a will that "my just debts be paid" does not ordinarily bind his half interest in the community estate to pay the entire community debts. However, the husband could make this provision, and the will is an excellent means of communicating his wishes. On the other hand, will provisions that are unclear may cause confusion, delays, and unnecessary expense.

For example, the phrase "my just debts be paid" may be interpreted as a requirement for the executor to pay off installment debts and long-term mortgage obligations immediately. The careful attorney will avoid this danger by providing that the executor shall not be required to pay debts prior to maturity but may extend or renew any debt upon such terms and for such time as he deems best. Thus, the will should explicitly state the intention of the testator. Does he wish the home to pass to the wife burdened with the mortgage or with the mortgage paid, if there are assets to satisfy the mortgage?

*Funeral Expenses*

Occasionally a testator will include detailed funeral arrangements in his will. If the testator feels strongly about some special funeral arrangements he should communicate his feelings to some member of the family, because the will is often not readily accessible at the time of death.

Funeral expenses and items incident thereto, such as tombstones, grave markers, crypts, or burial plots, are chargeable against the estate of the decedent, and no part thereof is to be charged against the community share of a surviving spouse. As a matter of public policy, such expenses are granted a high priority for payment. If the testator does not have burial insurance and if he has not otherwise provided for their payment in his will, then funeral expenses will be paid out of such assets as are available in the estate. If prior arrangements have not been made, emotional factors at the time of death can cause excessive funeral expenses.

### *Estate and Inheritance Taxes*

Just as funeral expenses are a kind of involuntary debt against the estate, so are taxes due because of death. The federal estate taxes and the State of Texas inheritance taxes may well be, and in many instances are, the largest costs chargeable to the estate. The reader should carefully review Chapters 5 and 6 for a detailed explanation of this subject.

It is the obligation of the executor to pay such taxes as are due. Here again, the testator may have made provisions to satisfy death taxes. If not, then the executor must look first to any available cash. If there is none, or if the cash is insufficient, then he must sell securities or other liquid assets to provide the necessary amount. Failure to provide funds for the payment of taxes may destroy the intention of the testator regarding beneficiaries.

Many people may not have much cash, but they are wealthy "on paper"; that is, they may own a farm or ranch or other assets that are considerably enhanced in value. The father may wish to leave such assets to his wife or children or both. If, at his death, the size of the estate is such that several thousand dollars in taxes are due, then the only alternative may be to sell all or a portion of the assets to raise the necessary funds.

The situation may arise where the deceased left sufficient assets to pay all the death taxes and other costs and requested that specific bequests be made. For example, suppose the home, personal effects, and life insurance proceeds go to the wife, the farm or ranch to the boys, and stocks and bonds to the daughters. Does the testator intend that such person receive the net interest, or does he intend that such interest bear its proportionate share of death taxes? The will should be clear and explicit with respect to the intention.

Normally testators wish the proceeds of insurance to pass to named beneficiaries in a net amount; thus, it is well to provide in the will that neither taxes nor debts are to be charged against any policies of insurance or the proceeds of such policies.

*Planning for the Payment of Debts and Taxes*

There are steps that may be taken to minimize probate costs, provide for the payment of debts, and reduce estate and inheritance taxes. A few important suggestions are listed here.

1. A current will, expertly drafted, may clarify many of the problems and, in addition, effect substantial tax savings.
2. A buy-sell agreement funded with life insurance is usually ideal where the testator is a member of a partnership or a closely-held business.
3. A mortgage cancellation policy on the home assures the home remaining intact.
4. Sufficient life insurance to pay all or some debts, cost of probate, and taxes offsets such costs.
5. Investment in other liquid assets that are readily marketable—such as stocks, bonds and savings—can provide necessary immediate cash.
6. Endowment insurance on the children, designed to mature at the time they are ready for college, will insure future security.
7. Gifts to children or grandchildren, directly or through trusts, may save or defer taxes, however, check with your counsel for any generation-skipping transfer tax problems.
8. A consistent program of saving also insures future security.
9. Careful selection of an independent executor with knowledge, skill, permanency, and financial responsibility is necessary because of the complicated nature of many estates. Selection of the executor may dictate the use of such professional help as a bank trust department.
10. Contracting during lifetime for only those obligations that can be paid without financial strain minimizes after-death indebtedness.
11. Consideration of educational, religious, or other charitable institutions as the ultimate beneficiary of the estate is particularly appropriate for a family without children. Even though the survivor may have the benefit of the estate for life, if title rests ultimately in a charity, tax savings may be substantial, since gifts to charity are generally tax free.

Before embarking on any or a combination of these suggestions as part of a formal estate plan, the advice of competent counsel should be sought.

## *Summary*

An unchangeable fact of our existence seems to be death, debts, and taxes. How debts and taxes are paid after death varies in direct proportion to the thought and planning given to them before death. A person who does not avail himself of the wealth of professional estate-planning talent available today is indeed unwise.

There is no substitute for competent legal advice. Home-drawn or do-it-yourself wills usually cause endless litigation and can penalize the family by higher costs and increased taxes. One improper sentence in a will may cause the entire estate to be taxed to the surviving spouse, and thus destroy the great advantages that are legally available.

The fee for an attorney to prepare a will which makes proper provision for payment of the debts created by the maker is small compared to the savings effected and the avoidance of costly delays in probate administration.

# 5

# Federal Estate Tax

When first enacted in 1916, the federal estate tax affected only families of great wealth. Since that time it has grown in scope until it is often the most formidable claim upon an estate. The federal estate tax affects more and more estates and is a significant factor in estate planning.

Legislative changes in the 1980s have made great changes in the law of federal estate taxation, and those changes will affect future estate planning. With proper planning under the law, fewer estates will pay federal estate taxes and significant estate tax deferral will be feasible.

Those alert to the effects of the estate tax take steps during their lives to minimize its impact and make preparation for payment of it. The federal government approves, indeed encourages, proper tax planning, and rewards with substantial savings those who act to minimize the tax. We all face income taxes annually, but estate taxes are faced after death—a time everyone tends to regard as too remote for present consideration. This chapter is written to familiarize the reader with the federal estate tax—the way it will affect an estate and how to prepare for it.

## Federal Transfer Tax

To understand how the federal estate tax works, it is necessary to realize that the estate tax is part of an overall federal transfer tax scheme which includes both gift taxes and estate taxes. There is a unified rate of tax for all taxable transfers, whether during a lifetime or at death, and there is a unified credit which makes a certain portion of those taxable transfers exempt from taxation. The unified credit can be used to avoid both gift tax during life and estate tax at death, but to the extent that the unified credit has been used during a lifetime, the amount of credit effectively available at death is reduced.

## What Is the Gross Estate?

The federal estate tax is imposed on the transfer of a decedent's property to his beneficiaries. The tax is based on the fair market value of the estate at the time of the decedent's death or, at the option of the taxpayer, on the fair market value of the estate six months after the date of death (the "alternate valuation date"). In addition, there is a special valuation procedure for farm and certain other real property used in a trade or business which may be elected in certain limited circumstances. In a community property estate the decedent's estate includes the entire value of all his separate property, as well as his one-half interest in all community property.

The value of the estate for tax purposes includes many things besides the property owned outright by the decedent (such as real property, stocks, bonds, cash, life insurance, certain employee benefits, and personal effects) at the time of his death. The testator should be aware that the following items may be included in the value of the estate for tax purposes:

1. *Insurance on the decedent's life in which he possessed any "incident of ownership" at the time of his death.* In addition to actual ownership of the policy, an incident of ownership includes the right to change the beneficiary, the right to borrow against the policy, or other similar rights available under an insurance policy.
2. *Property which the decedent conveyed during his lifetime.* Certain gifts made during a lifetime which are in excess of the annual exclusion amount (that is, gifts which are subject to gift tax) are included as part of the taxable estate. All gifts of life insurance made within three years of death are also included as part of the taxable estate.
3. *Property transferred by owner during his life but in which he retains certain rights.* These rights include the right to use the property for life, to revoke the transfer, to designate who should possess or enjoy the property, or in certain circumstances to vote stock which has been transferred. Where such transfer does not take effect until after the owner's death, it is also included in the estate.
4. *The decedent's interest in property owned by him and others as joint tenants with the rights of survivorship.*

5. *Certain property which the decedent held the right to direct the disposition.*

6. *The decedent's interest in employee benefit plans and certain other employee benefits.*

7. *Property in which the holder transfers to a family member a disproportionately large share of the potential appreciation in such interest while retaining an interest in the enterprise. This can occur when the decedent, in attempting to freeze the value of his business, surrenders his common stock to the company in exchange for both voting preferred and common stock, and subsequently transfers the common stock to a family member.*

From the foregoing it can be seen that determining what property constitutes a part of the decedent's estate and the value of that property for tax purposes can be complex.

### *Tax Rates*

The federal estate tax is a progressive tax much like the income tax. The rate increases with the value of the estate. Because of the unified credit discussed previously, a certain portion of an estate is exempt from taxation. Table 5-1 shows the exempt portion of an estate and the rate structure for the years 1988 and beyond.

If, for example, an individual died in 1988, the first $600,000 of his estate will be exempt from taxation. Any excess above that amount will be taxed at an effective rate no lower than 37% and no higher than 55%. As of 1993, the maximum rate is 50%. See footnote (2) to Table 5-1 for certain exceptions to the aforementioned rates.

### *Deductions*

Funeral expenses, administration expenses (such as accountant's fees, attorney's fees, costs of property management, and so on), and claims and debts against the estate may be deducted from the gross estate. What is left is the "net taxable estate." In community property estates the decedent's estate may deduct only half of the community debts and obligations.

In addition, a deduction referred to as the marital deduction is allowed for the value of certain property included in the gross estate which passes in a qualifying manner from the decedent to or for the benefit of the surviving spouse. This deduction is unlimited for all property so passing to the surviving spouse. Thus, it is conceivable that federal estate tax may be entirely eliminated in the estate of the first spouse to die if a proper estate plan is used (see Chapter 7). An unlimited deduction is also allowed for the value of all property left to charity.

### Table 5-1
### Federal Estate Exemption and Rate Structure

| Year | Minimum Effective Rate (%) | On Transfers Exceeding ($)[1,2] | Maximum Rate (%)[2] | On Transfers Exceeding ($) |
|---|---|---|---|---|
| 1988 | 37 | 600,000 | 55 | 3,000,000 |
| 1993 or thereafter | 37 | 600,000 | 50 | 2,500,000 |

[1] Exempt portion of estate.
[2] An extra 5% tax is imposed upon cumulative taxable transfers between $10,000,000 and $21,040,000 ($18,340,000 after 1992). This will eliminate the graduated tax rates that are applicable to transfers up to $3,000,000 and the unified transfer tax credit ($600,000 exemption). Thus, if cumulative transfers beginning in 1988 through 1992 exceed $21,040,000, a flat tax rate of 55% will apply to all such transfers. Beginning in 1993, if cumulative transfers exceed $18,340,000, a flat tax rate of 50% will apply to all such transfers.

## What Is the Net Taxable Estate?

After the gross estate has been reduced by all deductions (including marital deductions and any charitable deductions), what remains is the taxable estate. This is the amount against which the tax rates apply.

In determining the tax payable by a decedent's estate, four credits are allowed. A credit is a direct reduction of the tax (as distinguished from a deduction). The most important credit is, of course, the unified credit discussed previously. This credit is available to everyone and determines the exempt portion of the estate, which is shown in Table 5-1. The unified credit and the resultant tax-exempt portion of an estate are important in estate tax planning and can be used to reduce overall estate taxes. Other credits include:

1. *State death taxes.* A credit is allowed against the estate tax for the amount of any estate, inheritance, or similar tax paid to any state or the District of Columbia with respect to property included in the gross estate. The amount of this credit is subject to various limitations.

2. *Prior estate taxes paid.* A credit is allowed against the estate tax for any federal estate tax paid on transfer of property to the decedent from a prior decedent (who died within a period up to 10 years before or within 2 years after the present decedent's death). It is not necessary that the transferred property be identified in the present decedent's estate, or that it be in existence at the time of his death. The maximum credit is allowed for 2 years after the prior decedent's death; after that, the credit is reduced by 20% every 2 years. In the third and fourth years, therefore, only 80% of the maximum credit is allowed, and this reduces to 20% in the ninth and tenth year. There is no credit after 10 years.

3. *Foreign death taxes.* A credit is allowed against the estate tax for any estate, inheritance, or similar tax actually paid to a foreign country by the decedent's estate. Again, such credit is subject to various limitations set out in the Internal Revenue Code.

### Minimizing the Tax

Proper estate planning minimizes the tax payments. It is possible to use both the exemption and the unlimited marital deduction to minimize estate tax and to defer that tax until the death of the surviving spouse. Various means can be used to accomplish this goal, one of which includes the creation of trusts in the will which take maximum advantage of the estate tax laws and provide for the descendants of the decedent ultimately to receive the property after the surviving spouse (who has had the benefit of the estate for the rest of his or her life) has died. An example of a tax minimization estate plan for a married couple is one in which the estate is split into two parts. One part is held in trust for the benefit of the surviving spouse and on his or her death is distributed to the children. This trust is funded with assets the value of which equals the exempt portion of the estate in the year of death (see Table 5–1).

This trust is subject to estate tax, but no tax is incurred since the value of the assets does not exceed the exempt portion of the estate. The advantage of this trust is that it is not taxable in the surviving spouse's estate when he or she later dies. It is thus known as a "bypass trust," since it bypasses the surviving spouse's estate and is passed on to the children. The remainder of the estate will pass in such a manner that it qualifies for the marital deduction. Thus, estate taxes can be avoided in the estate of the first spouse to die and maximum use of the unified credit can reduce total tax liability upon the survivor's subsequent death.

Although the use of trusts can frequently help minimize estate taxes, the generation-skipping transfer tax should be considered in planning bypass and other trusts that will be held for the benefit of several generations. The extremely complex provisions of this tax essentially prevent an individual from avoiding estate tax on property passing from generation to generation. At some point, tax on that property will be imposed. There are various exceptions to the generation-skipping transfer tax in addition to a $1,000,000 exemption per transferor; however, it remains a factor in estate tax planning.

### Paying the Tax

As a general rule, the estate tax must be paid in cash nine months after the date of death. The cash requirement and other cash demands upon the estate make it desirable to prepare a proper estimate of the tax liability and proper provisions for payment. "Liquidity" is the term applied to provision for payment of the federal estate tax and other liabilities. Planning liquidity carefully will ensure that the estate executor will not be forced to raise tax funds by selling assets at an unfavorable time or that are difficult to sell. It should be noted that the new unlimited marital deduction that allows for deferral of all taxes until the death of the surviving spouse has to a certain extent removed the liquidity problem in the estate of the first spouse to die.

Under certain circumstances, the executor of an estate may obtain an extension of time within which to pay the estate tax. The Internal Revenue Service can allow for "reasonable cause" up to 10 years to pay the tax with interest (the interest rate varies in relation to market conditions). In addition, a 15-year installment payment plan is available if a specific portion of the estate consists of certain assets such as a closely held business. Part of the estate tax bears interest at a rate of 4%. The interest rate on the balance varies in relation to the market conditions. The closely held business exception may apply in certain circumstances where it is not readily apparent, such as ownership of ranches, producing oil leases (working interests), and similar properties which are an active trade or business. The reasonable-cause provision is frequently granted and consent is generally given if a sufficient payment is made on the tax liability equal to the value of the liquid assets of the estate.

### *Summary*

Death and taxes are said to be inevitable. The federal government gives each person an opportunity to plan his estate in a way that minimizes the effect of the federal estate tax. Since the building of an estate is difficult, everyone should become familiar with the provisions of the federal estate tax and prepare for it.

# 6

# The Texas Inheritance Tax

The State of Texas has imposed a death tax since 1907. The tax is known as the Texas inheritance tax, and it is administered by the Comptroller of Public Accounts in Austin. Effective September 1, 1981, the tax was substantially revised and simplified by the Texas Legislature.

*The Tax Prior to September 1, 1981*

The Texas inheritance tax, prior to the 1981 simplification, actually consisted of two separate taxes: (1) the "basic" inheritance tax, and (2) the "additional" inheritance tax (commonly referred to as the "pickup" tax). The basic tax was computed on the value of property within the jurisdiction of the State of Texas and passing from a decedent to a beneficiary by will or by the laws of inheritance. The tax was computed based upon the total value of property received by each beneficiary and the exemptions and tax rates favored family members. Property passing to a spouse, parent, child, or grandchild was taxed at the lowest rate, while property passing to a nonrelative was taxed at the highest rate. A minimum of $200,000 in property could pass to the "favored" class of beneficiaries free from tax.

The "additional" inheritance tax simply was intended to take advantage of the federal estate tax provision which allows a credit against the federal tax for death tax paid to any state. Of course, the federal law limits the amount of this credit and provides a table of the maximum credit allowable to estates of various sizes. The "additional" inheritance tax in Texas was the excess of the federal credit over the basic inheritance tax amount. Since the federal credit for state death taxes reduces the amount payable to the federal government, this additional inheritance tax (the "pick-up" tax) did not increase the combined federal and state tax payable by an estate. If the basic inheritance tax equalled or exceeded the federal credit, the "additional" tax was zero.

### The New Texas Inheritance Tax and
### Generation-Skipping Transfer Tax System

Effective for decedents dying after August 31, 1981, the basic inheritance tax was repealed, and the additional or pick-up tax was revised. Essentially, the State of Texas now imposes an inheritance tax equal to the maximum amount of the federal credit for state death taxes (we will refer to this as the "federal credit"). The tax is imposed on Texas residents. The tax is also imposed on nonresidents (including aliens) owning property located in Texas. And, to the extent that the federal "generation-skipping" transfer tax is imposed upon property located in Texas, the Texas inheritance tax will also pick up that federal credit.

In the case of residents of Texas with property subject to a death tax imposed by another state or states, the Texas tax provides for apportionment of the credit among the various states. Essentially, the Texas portion of the credit is the ratio of Texas property to the decedent's total property. For this purpose, a resident's Texas property includes real estate and tangible property actually located in Texas and intangible personal property (stocks, bonds, notes, etc.) wherever located. To the extent property is community property of the decedent and his or her spouse, only one-half is subject to tax.

Real property and tangible personal property owned by nonresidents but located in Texas are subject to tax. Again, the tax will be a percentage of the federal credit based upon Texas property in relation to total property.

### Filing the Inheritance Tax and
### Generation-Skipping Transfer Tax Returns

The Comptroller currently requires the filing of a Texas Inheritance Tax Return by the estate of every decedent with property in Texas if a federal estate tax return is required to be filed. The return is a simple, one-page form due nine months from the date of death. A copy of the federal estate tax return (Form 706) must be attached to the inheritance tax return. A payment of a generation-skipping transfer tax must be accompanied by a copy of the federal generation-skipping transfer tax return (Form 706-B). In addition, copies of federal "acceptance letters" or audit changes must be sent to the Comptroller within 30 days of receipt. The Comptroller also has the power to exchange information with the Internal Revenue Service in determining the value of an estate.

The executor or administrator of an estate is legally responsible for filing the return and paying the tax. Penalties and interest will be assessed for late payment of the tax, although the penalties may be waived for "reasonable cause." An approved extension of time to file the federal return will also extend the due date of the Texas return. The executor or administrator is required to notify the Comptroller within 30 days after an extension is granted by the Internal Revenue Service. Further, effective for inheritance tax due after July 21, 1987, an estate may request an extension of time to pay the inheritance tax for good cause if the federal estate tax is extended. The extension request must be made to the comptroller on or before the original due date for payment after tax.

It is important to note that an executor generally may not transfer or deliver the decedent's property to the beneficiaries until the inheritance tax has been paid. If the executor or administrator transfers any of the decedent's property to any person without having paid the inheritance tax, the executor or administrator is personally liable for any tax, penalty, and interest to the extent of the value of the property transferred.

## The Effects of the 1981 Changes

The 1981 revision of the Texas inheritance tax was very significant. In addition to reducing the amount of inheritance taxes, compliance with the Texas inheritance tax provisions has been greatly simplified. Under prior law, executors or administrators and their professional advisers were required to prepare a tax return similar in size and complexity to the federal estate tax return. And, since there were differences between the federal and state rules, the Texas return required substantial time, effort, and expense. In many cases, of course, the additional effort was somewhat nonproductive, since the ultimate tax due the State of Texas was simply the federal credit amount (due to the "additional" tax computation). Now, the tax paid to Texas will reduce the federal tax dollar for dollar and, essentially, does not create any additional tax burden upon estate beneficiaries.

The impact of the 1981 changes is especially significant for married couples due to the federal marital deduction rules included in the Economic Recovery Tax Act of 1981 (ERTA). Under those rules (discussed in Chapter 7), an individual's estate will incur no federal tax if sufficient property is left to his or her surviving spouse. Thus, since no federal tax is incurred, no inheritance tax will be due the State of Texas.

Another effect of ERTA is the increased amount of property which is exempt from federal estate tax. Beginning in 1987, the first $600,000 in an estate is free from federal tax and, therefore, is free from Texas inheritance tax.

## *Summary*

The 1981 changes in the Texas inheritance tax law, when combined with the 1981 changes in the federal estate tax law, created a truly simplified inheritance tax system for Texas residents and nonresidents with property subject to Texas jurisdiction.

# 7

# What Is the Marital Deduction?

"Marital deduction" is an estate tax term that only applies to married couples, and it is a fairly complex subject. However, it can be critically important to people of moderate-to-substantial means, and some of the most helpful "good news" in the Economic Recovery Tax Act of 1981 (ERTA) involves the marital deduction, so a working knowledge of the basic principles is essential.

*History of the Marital Deduction*

The marital deduction concept is easier to grasp if you know something about its history and how it came to be.

In Chapter 1 the reader learned about community property and separate property, and probably quickly perceived the estate tax advantage for residents of a "community property" state versus a "common law" state where assets acquired during marriage are often considered to be the husband's "separate property." (If the husband in a community property state dies, only his half of the community property is subject to estate tax.) In 1942, Congress undertook to eliminate a number of tax inequalities between community property and common law states. Its approach was to provide that 100% of the community property would be taxed if the husband died (with certain exceptions).

That approach created as many problems as it solved, so in 1948 that provision was repealed and the first marital deduction was enacted. Simply stated, that law authorized an estate tax deduction for property passing to a surviving spouse, with a limit equal to one-half the value of the decedent's separate property. Thus, in a common law state the husband could leave up to half of his property to his spouse, take the estate tax marital deduction and achieve the same tax result as a deceased husband in a community property state. For residents of community property states, the marital deduction applied to a spouse's separate property.

The Tax Reform Act of 1976 modified the estate tax to a "unified transfer tax system," and for the first time the marital deduction could be taken to a limited extent for community property passing to a surviving spouse.

Then, with ERTA came a sweeping change in the form of the "unlimited marital deduction." Now, one spouse may transfer any amount of property, either during life or at death, to the other spouse without tax and *without regard to whether community property or separate property is being transferred*. In tax language we say that there is an unlimited marital deduction for property transferred to a spouse for gift tax purposes on lifetime transfers, and for estate tax purposes on deathtime transfers, emphasizing again that it no longer matters whether the transferred property is separate or community. In fact, for a lifetime gift to a spouse, a gift tax return does not have to be filed, regardless of the value of the gift.

### The Marital Deduction and Tax Planning

Now let us address how the marital deduction fits into tax planning for married couples. In how large or how small an estate is it important? May or should trusts be used? Can it be overutilized? When would it be important to use the marital deduction for lifetime gifts?

### Unified Credit Coordination

If, after reading about the unlimited marital deduction, the reader jumps to the conclusion that one should simply leave everything to one's spouse and there will be no tax problems, then the importance of coordinating the marital deduction with the unified credit (explained in Chapter 5) will have been overlooked. Depending on the size of the estate, it could be an expensive mistake.

Perhaps a series of simple bar charts will help illustrate how the marital deduction and unified credit should be planned for together, and the dollar values where marital deduction planning becomes important. The illustrations are cast in terms of the husband dying first (since actuarially women outlive men, but the principles are equally important if the wife dies first).

Figure 7–1 assumes a husband and wife with $600,000 of community property. Here, the husband's gross estate is $300,000, and his estate tax is zero; however, this zero-tax results from the unified credit without having to use the marital deduction. If he leaves everything to his wife outright (the dashed line indicates the addition to her estate), at her subsequent death her gross estate will be $600,000. Again, the tax will be zero due to the unified credit, and the full value of the family assets will pass to the next generation without any transfer tax.

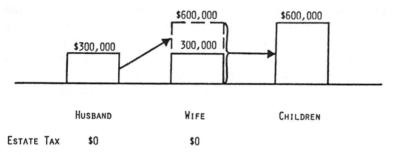

**Figure 7-1.** Husband and wife with $600,000 in community property.

Figure 7–2 assumes a couple of greater means, with $1.2 million in community property. This husband's gross estate is $600,000, and again his estate tax will be zero due to the unified credit and regardless of marital deduction. If he leaves his entire estate outright to the wife, her gross estate will be $1.2 million, on which a tax of $235,000 will be owed, thus shrinking the family assets passing to the children to $965,000.

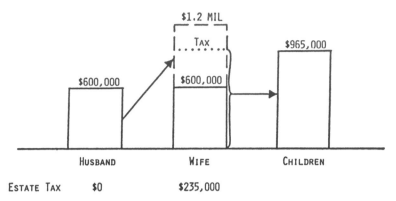

Figure 7-2. Husband and wife with $1.2 million in community property.

Figure 7–3 illustrates how the same couple could avoid any estate tax at either death by use of a "bypass trust," the most frequently used estate-planning vehicle in the past, and which still has utility. Here, instead of leaving his estate outright to the wife, the husband has created a trust for her; she can receive all of the income during her lifetime and the principal can be used for her support if needed—literally the same financial benefits she would have if the husband left his estate to her outright. But, the trust "bypasses" the wife's estate for tax purposes. Her tax is then zero due to the unified credit,

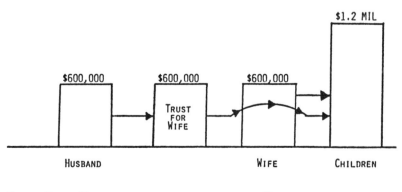

Figure 7-3. Use of the bypass trust in a husband-and-wife community estate of $1.2 million.

and the full $1.2 million of family assets can be passed to the next generation without any transfer tax.

So far, these hypothetical couples have been able to achieve very attractive tax results without using marital deduction planning. However, for those with family assets in excess of $1.2 million, the marital deduction becomes very important. Figure 7–4 assumes a couple with $2 million of community property. The husband's gross estate will be $1 million, and if he leaves it to the wife outright, his estate tax will be zero ($600,000 is exempt from tax under the unified credit, and the excess qualifies for the marital deduction). However, the wife's gross estate will then be $2 million, which will be reduced by a $588,000 estate tax, with a net amount of $1.41 million passing to the children.

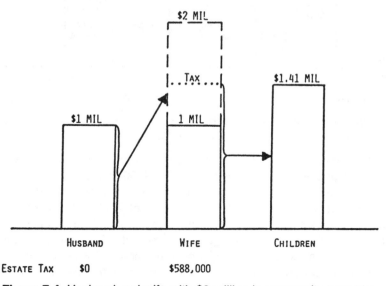

**Figure 7-4.** Husband and wife with $2 million in community property.

Figure 7–5 illustrates how this couple could use a combination of the marital deduction and the unified credit to increase the net amount given to the children by $268,000. Here, the husband places an amount equal to the $600,000 exemption equivalent in a bypass trust for the wife and leaves the excess to her (outright, for simplicity in this example), thus qualifying for the marital deduction so that his tax is zero. The wife's gross estate, then, is $1.4 million, and her estate tax is only $320,000 (a $268,000 saving) because the husband's estate is not "stacked" on top of hers. Thus, the next generation receives $1.68 million instead of only $1.41 million.

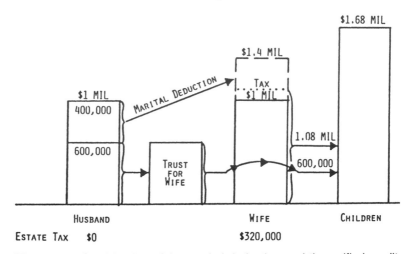

**Figure 7-5.** Combination of the marital deduction and the unified credit increases the net amount received by offspring.

It is important to note that this use of the marital deduction did not completely avoid estate tax on the $400,000 excess over the exemption equivalent in the husband's estate—it simply deferred the tax on that amount until the wife's subsequent death. But tax deferral also means savings, because money which would have otherwise been paid for estate taxes at the husband's death is still available throughout the wife's lifetime, producing income for her benefit. If a 10% annual return were available and the wife survived for 10 years, that would mean a total of $400,000 of additional income for her.

*Marital Deduction Trusts*

The marital deduction bequest does not have to go to the spouse outright but can be left in trust provided certain requirements are met. Trusts are used basically for two purposes: (1) to provide management of assets, and (2) tax reasons. A marital deduction trust usually combines both of these objectives.

The one essential ingredient of all marital deduction trust arrangements is that the trust must be structured so that it will be taxable in the surviving spouse's estate; otherwise, a marital deduction will not be allowed in the first spouse's estate.

There are three kinds of marital deduction trusts, the first two of which were used before ERTA and are still workable vehicles in appropriate instances:

1. A marital deduction is allowed for a "power-of-appointment trust" if (a) the surviving spouse receives all of the income at least annually during lifetime, and (b) has the power (whether exercised or not) to specify by will who receives the trust when the surviving spouse dies (which is a "power of appointment" in legal terms).

2. An "estate trust" also qualifies for the marital deduction and differs from the power of appointment trust in that income may be accumulated if the trust, including accumulated income, must be distributed to the spouse's estate (and be taxed there) when he or she dies. Sometimes a combination is used where accumulated income must be distributed to a spouse's estate, and the principal is subject to the spouse's power of appointment.

3. ERTA allows a marital deduction for a trust containing "qualified terminable interest property," commonly known by acronym as a "QTIP trust." For the trust to qualify: (a) the spouse must receive all of the income at least annually; (b) no one, including the spouse, may have the power to appoint (transfer) the trust property away from the spouse during lifetime; and (c) the executor must make an appropriate election on the estate tax return.

The unique feature of a QTIP trust is that the spouse creating the trust may specify who will receive the QTIP property when the surviving spouse dies, but the QTIP property will be taxed in the surviving spouse's estate.

The surviving spouse's estate may recover from the transferees the estate tax paid by virtue of including the QTIP property in the surviving spouse's estate.

Various objectives, such as the desire for management of assets and tax implications, will dictate whether or not to use a marital deduction trust, and if so, what kind. However, since 1981, a larger menu of alternatives is available. Among other things, if a QTIP trust passes to charity after the death of the surviving spouse, it is now possible to avoid any transfer tax at all on the property.

### Factors Considered in Marital Deduction Planning

A number of factors should be taken into account in determining how and to what extent the marital deduction is used.

First, there are two ways to achieve coordination of the marital deduction and the unified credit. Under the basic plan diagrammed in Figure 7–5, the bypass trust is not going to exceed the $600,000 exemption equivalent. One way, commonly called the "cutback marital deduction bequest," is a specific bequest on a formula basis to the surviving spouse to take advantage of the marital deduction, with the balance (or residue) of the estate, which will be $600,000, passing to the bypass trust. Another way is to make a specific bequest of the $600,000 exemption equivalent to the bypass trust, and leave the residue to the spouse. An oversimplified statement of the cutback bequest is "I give my spouse that amount which would cut my estate tax back to zero, and I give the residue of my estate to my Trustee." A similarly oversimplified statement of the specific bequest to the trust is "I give my Trustee an amount equal to the exemption equivalent of the unified credit for estate tax purposes, and I give the residue to my spouse."

Parenthetically, it should be noted that either method can achieve zero tax at the first spouse's death.

Both of these bequests are formula-type arrangements, and the reader will find that the will language is considerably more complicated, as it must be to achieve the desired results by formula and track the exacting language of the Internal Revenue Code.

Which approach to use is generally dictated by income tax considerations. The principal concern is that distribution of assets (other than cash) in satisfaction of a specific bequest will invoke complex income tax considerations involving realization of gain or loss. Since either approach is determined under a formula, it will probably involve distribution of assets other than cash, and if the estate has been open for a period of time, those assets will likely have gone up or down in value.

Therefore, in a very large estate it is usually desirable to make the specific bequests to the trust, since the bequest should not exceed $600,000, and expose less assets to gain-or-loss income tax problems.

Another income tax consideration involves the extent to which a distribution of the estate will carry out taxable income to the distributees. Although this subject is outside the scope of this chapter, the reader should bear in mind that it will influence the planning process when wills are drawn, as well as timing considerations when an estate is distributed.

Second, we should ask ourselves whether we should *always* opt for maximum tax deferral by always using the marital deduction to the fullest extent possible.

Assets placed in the bypass trust are sheltered from estate tax at the second spouse's death, and the shelter applies to appreciation in value occurring after the first spouse dies, as well as to the initial value placed in the Trust. The alternative to maximum deferral is to pay tax at the first spouse's death (in effect prepay tax which could be deferred by use of the marital deduction) in order to shelter future appreciation from estate tax at the second spouse's death. So, if the family holdings include assets with substantial appreciation potential, full use of the marital deduction might not be the most advantageous result. Furthermore, the taxable income from the family holdings should be considered. In a large estate, if most of the assets are left to the surviving spouse to obtain a maximum marital deduction, he or she will be taxable on all of the income, and if the income is more than the spouse needs, it cannot be shifted without tax consequences to family members in lower tax brackets.

In the past, fairly fixed patterns of marital deduction planning could be established. One basic tenet was that maximum tax results could be achieved if both spouses' taxable estates could be kept approximately equal. But now, in determining to what extent the marital deduction should be used, there are many more variables that cannot be foreseen precisely. The time value of money is an essential part of the equation in comparing the benefits of tax deferral against the benefits of tax-sheltering future appreciation in a bypass trust. On the deferral side, the compound income from the deferred tax can produce high figures, particularly when interest rates are high. In considering the sheltering of future appreciation from tax, compound growth of tax-sheltered assets can be significant, and future taxes should be discounted to present value. The ultimate result of mathematical projections brings life expectancies into play, and people's lives are usually longer or shorter than their actuarial expectancies. So, the reader will find that in the estate-planning process the analysis of his or her own estate will probably be sophisticated, and that in administering an estate important decisions—not always easy ones—will need to be made.

Third, future flexibility is vital in estate planning. How can options be preserved with regard to the marital deduction?

To obtain the marital deduction for a QTIP trust, the executor must elect on the estate tax return for it to apply. One source of flexibility is in the Internal Revenue Code itself, which provides the executor may elect that only a fractional, or percentile, share of the marital deduction bequest shall qualify for the marital deduction. Thus, the will may include different provisions to be applied to the portion of the marital deduction which is not elected, with differing tax consequences, for example, tax-sheltered bypass provisions. Another alternative provides that if a surviving spouse disclaims all or part of the marital deduction bequest, it will pass in a manner that achieves different tax results, perhaps to a trust sheltered from tax at the second spouse's death, or a Trust from which income can be sprinkled to other family members.

## Lifetime Gifts

As stated earlier in this chapter, the unlimited marital deduction is available for lifetime gifts to a spouse. While there are not now as many tax-motivated reasons for lifetime giving between spouses due to the fact the tax can be reduced to zero at the first death, there is still much more freedom to make such gifts for whatever reasons—other than taxes—a spouse may want to.

One instance where tax planning could motivate a lifetime gift from spouse to spouse is where one spouse has substantially more property than the other plus a longer life expectancy. Figure 7–6 shows a husband with a $300,000 gross estate, and a wife several years younger than he, who because of an inheritance, has a gross estate of $900,000 (on which there will be an estate tax of $114,000 at her death). If the wife makes a $300,000 lifetime gift to the husband, his gross estate becomes $600,000, on which there will be

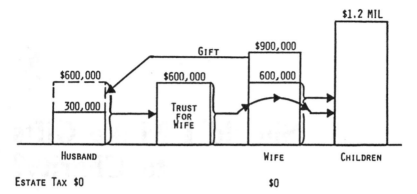

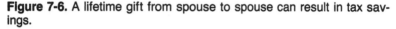

**Figure 7-6.** A lifetime gift from spouse to spouse can result in tax savings.

no tax due to the unified credit. He could leave it to a bypass trust for the wife so that her gross estate is reduced to $600,000 by the lifetime gift, and the entire family assets of $1.2 million can be passed to the children tax-free under the unified credit. The result is the same as in Figure 7–3, where the spouses had equal estates.

One important limitation on this plan was imposed by ERTA. If the donee spouse dies within two years of the gift, there will be no step-up in basis of the gifted property for income tax purposes. See Chapter 3 regarding the effect of valuation on basis.

### *Summary*

This chapter covers an extensive subject in summary form and contains some oversimplification of the complexities experienced in estate planning for the marital deduction or during the administration of an estate. However, a basic understanding of the fundamentals of the marital deduction is important in the planning of estates of married couples.

# 8

# Should I Make Gifts to Charity?

Charitable donations have become an accepted and sometimes expected part of today's society. The decision as to whether or not to make gifts to charity (either during one's lifetime or by will) is a personal matter. Obviously, the selection of the charity, the timing of the gift, the amount of the gift, and the type of property given will depend upon the individual's attitude, desires, and financial resources and responsibilities.

Once the decision has been made to contribute to charity (or at least to consider it), the tax effects of the gift become important: income, gift, and estate tax deductions are allowable for certain charitable gifts. Often, income taxes are the largest item of an individual's budget, and in many instances, the estate and inheritance tax bill is the largest expense of the deceased's estate. If a person can accomplish his charitable objectives and reduce his tax bill, he is apt to be a "cheerful giver."

## Gifts of Cash or Property

When considering some sort of charitable contribution by will, most people think in terms of a cash donation of a fixed amount, with the bulk of the estate passing to the surviving family. Under such circumstances the entire amount of the charitable bequest is usually deductible for federal estate tax and state inheritance tax purposes.

Often, however, cash will be needed in the estate to defray the costs of administration and taxes. Payment of the charitable legacies in cash could produce a cash shortage, necessitating the sale of other properties. The estate may be composed primarily of real estate or closely held corporate stock which may be nonliquid in the sense that they cannot be easily sold. Sale of those properties either to pay the charitable bequest or to restore cash used to pay the charity may not only be inconvenient, but may result in an income tax if the property sold has a fair market value in excess of the value of the property as reported for federal estate tax purposes. To avoid these problems, the individual may wish to bequeath other property instead of cash. The entire value of the property given will usually be tax deductible.

## Fixed Amount or Percentage

Instead of bequeathing a specific dollar amount or designated properties to charity, one may wish to consider giving a fixed percentage of his estate. If the will is drafted so that the charitable bequest is not burdened by administrative costs of the estate or other charges, the entire gift will usually be deductible for tax purposes. Another advantage of the percentage gift is an across-the-board reduction of the gift if the estate has a lower value than the donor expected.

## Trust Gifts

Family responsibilities may prevent a substantial outright gift by will to charity. However, family circumstances may make it possible to make a charitable bequest of an income right or of the remainder interest in certain properties. For example, the testator may wish to provide a source of income to his wife or to his parents, but would like the property ultimately to pass to charity. Or he may feel that adequate provision has been made for his children during minority and provide for an income right from property for a charity until the children become adults (at which time the property would pass to them).

By setting up a trust in his will to provide for current distributions to one party and ultimately the remainder interest in the trust property to another party, the testator may accomplish his objectives. A trust of this type is known as a charitable remainder trust or a charitable lead trust. In the former instance the testator could provide for trust distributions (a specified dollar amount or a specified percentage of the value of the property in the trust) to his wife or to his parents for life with the remainder of the property passing to charity upon their deaths. In the latter instance he could provide for trust distributions to the charity (a specified dollar amount or a specified percentage of the value of the property in the trust) until all of his children became adults, at which time the property in the trust would be delivered to them. Under either arrangement, the present value of the remainder interest or the income interest passing to charity will be deductible for estate tax purposes. Furthermore, as a result of the Economic Recovery Tax Act of 1981 (ERTA), if the testator's spouse is the sole beneficiary of the income interest with the remainder passing to charity, the *entire* gift may be deductible for federal estate tax purposes. Care must be exercised in drafting the will for the trust to meet applicable tax requirements.

### *Lifetime Gifts*

If a person has decided to make charitable contributions, it may be appropriate for him to consider making them while he is still living. The values of lifetime gifts to charities are fully deductible for gift tax purposes and, unlike most charitable gifts made by will, lifetime gifts to charity may result in an income tax deduction to the donor. Further, unlike taxable lifetime outright gifts made after the Tax Reform Act of 1976 (which are added back to "gross up" the donor's estate at his subsequent death for purposes of determining the federal estate tax rate applicable to his estate), lifetime charitable gifts (being nontaxable gifts) are not normally grossed up in the computation of the federal estate tax rate, and therefore, serve to reduce the applicable federal estate tax bracket.

For example, if a person wishes to give certain property to charity at his death, it may be desirable for him to establish a trust during his lifetime, reserving an income right from the trust (a specified dollar amount or a specified percentage of the value of the property in the trust) for himself with the remainder to go to charity at his death. Since the only gift is that of the remainder interest, and it is given to charity, there would be no gift tax. Because the property will pass to charity at his death, its value is deductible for estate tax purposes. The value of the remainder interest given to charity will usually be deductible for income tax purposes, subject to the income tax limitations on charitable deductions.

The amount of the income tax deduction varies with the length of time the charity must wait for the gift, the type of property given, the type of charity receiving the gift, and the amount of the income right retained by the donor; however, the donor's deduction is immediate so that spendable dollars in the year of the gift are increased and the donor will have an income right from the trust for the rest of his life.

Under such an arrangement, properties which have appreciated in value since the donor acquired them may be given to the trust. It may be better in some instances to contribute directly the trust properties that have increased in value rather than sell the properties first and then contribute cash to the trust. If the properties are sold by the donor, he will have to pay the capital gains tax and, thus, fewer dollars could pass to charity and a smaller charitable deduction would be available. If appreciated property is gifted to charity, the alternative minimum tax may apply after the Tax Reform Act of 1986 because of its classification of the untaxed appreciation on the asset contributed as an item of tax preference.

## Income Tax Deduction for Gifts

There are limitations on the amount of charitable gifts that are tax deductible within a given year. The limitations vary depending upon the type of property given and the type of charitable organization selected. Generally, cash gifts to public charities qualify for the largest deduction within a year. The size of charitable contributions in any particular year must be carefully planned if all of them are to be tax deductible. For example, if a gift to a charity is too large to be entirely deductible in one year, the excess portion can be carried forward to each of the next five years when it might be deductible by the donor. If the amount of the gift is too large to be completely deductible in the six-year period, it may be advisable for the charitable gift to be made over a period of years.

Thus, rather than giving a block of stock in one particular year, a smaller number of shares might be given over several years. Similarly, an undivided interest in real estate can be given periodically for the most income tax benefits.

### Gift of Life Insurance

There are, of course, other methods of making charitable contributions. One of these involves using life insurance. An individual may transfer to charity an existing life insurance policy and be entitled to a charitable deduction for its value (roughly, the cash surrender value of the policy). Subsequent premium payments by him may also be deductible for income tax purposes.

### Charitable Foundations

Prior to the Tax Reform Act of 1969, there had been a considerable growth in both the number and the activities of private charitable foundations. Under this procedure, an individual established a foundation either in the form of a charitable trust or a non-profit corporation. If properly established, the private foundation was tax exempt and contributions to it were deductible for income, gift, and estate tax purposes. By making his charitable contributions to the foundation, which could make investments without being taxed on the income and which could distribute the income to other charities, the individual maximized his potential for charitable giving.

Because of suspected widespread abuse with some private foundations, Congress in 1969 imposed substantial limitations upon the activities of private foundations. Because of the complexity of complying with these limitations, the establishment of small private foundations has declined. Despite these complexities, the establishment of a private foundation which is properly organized and operated may still be advantageous. By establishing a private foundation, the founders can, within certain limits, control the investment of the gifted funds and selection of the charitable recipients.

*Summary*

The manner in which charitable gifts can be most advantageously utilized by the individual depends on the amount and nature of his assets, as well as the relation of the income, gift and estate taxes to his own particular situation. Apart from tax advantages, charitable giving often makes good sense for family reasons. Coordination of charitable contributions with plans for individual and family economic and estate planning, and the tax effects thereof, often result in the maximum charitable and individual benefits.

# 9

# Should I Make a Will?

Most people work hard to acquire and keep property during their lifetimes. However, a surprisingly large number of people die without a will. Those people forfeit the right to determine the disposition of their property and fail to provide for their family's continued well-being. They die leaving the security of their family to chance and the disposition of their property to the law.

*Who Can and Should Make a Will*

The records of the probate courts in Texas show that wealthy people—people with property in excess of $500,000—usually recognize the value of planning their estate. Most of the persons who die without a will are the owners of modest or medium-sized estates. Yet, saving a dollar in a $100,000 estate means much more to that family than saving a dollar would to a family with a $1 million estate.

A will is a written instrument by which a person (a testator) disposes of his property effective at his death. It is always subject to change by the maker during his lifetime. It conveys no present interest in property or rights to any beneficiary until the maker's death. As a result a will can dispose of property acquired after the will was made.

Texas law gives to every person of sound mind who is at least 18 years old, or is or was lawfully married, or is a member of the armed forces at the time the will is made the right to make a will. This right carries with it the privilege of disposing of one's estate in any manner and to anyone. Texas law does not require that property be left to one's wife, children, parents, or any other person.

## Types of Wills

There are basically two types of wills provided for by Texas law. The most common type is the typewritten will, usually prepared by an attorney. For such a will to be valid it must be in writing and signed by the maker (testator) or by someone signing for him at his direction and in his presence. This form of will must be attested by two or more credible witnesses above the age of 14 years, who must also sign their names to the will in their own handwriting and in the presence of the person making the will. A witness should not be a beneficiary under the will. If the requirements for execution of the will and its attestation are not strictly complied with, the will is invalid and may be contested. Likewise, if the maker is not of sound mind or is acting under undue influence when the will is executed, it is invalid. Hence, it is advisable to have an attorney supervise the making and execution of a will to make certain all of the prerequisites for validity and the various formalities of execution have been complied with.

The other type of will commonly used in Texas is one which is written wholly in the handwriting of and signed by the testator. This is a "holographic" will and does not require witnesses in order to be valid. A typewritten instrument, or one written by someone other than the maker, is not a holographic will and must be properly executed and witnessed.

## Dying Without a Will

When a person dies in Texas without a will, the laws of Descent and Distribution determine who shall inherit his property and in what proportions the property shall be distributed. These laws also govern the distribution of property not disposed of by a decedent's will, either because the will does not cover all of the property or because it is invalid. Where there is a will, unless a contrary intention is plainly expressed or necessarily implied, it will be presumed that the maker intended to dispose of his entire estate according to its terms.

The properties disposed of by a decedent's will, or by the laws of Descent and Distribution, are only the decedent's separate property and his half interest in community property. Under the laws of Descent and Distribution the disposition of community and separate property differ. The disposition of community property will be the same whether the property is real estate or personal property. However, the disposition of separate property will differ depending upon whether the property is realty or personalty.

Figures 9-1 and 9-2 show how property not disposed of by a will is distributed to the heirs at law in Texas.

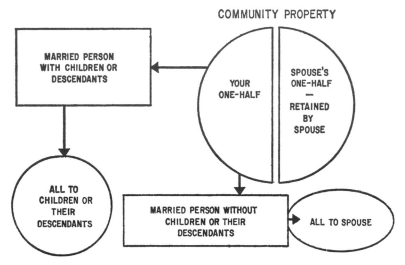

**Figure 9-1.** Community property distribution without a will.

This illustrated distribution of property is the will which the State of Texas has written for a person who does not take the opportunity to make his own. It is inflexible and does not take into account the individual needs and requirements of the various family members. If a father, owning only community property, dies without a will, his wife inherits nothing from him. If the mother's half of the community property and her widow's allowance for one year's support are not sufficient to support her, she will have to go to work or find other means of support, even though the father's half of the community property is not needed for the support of the children who receive it. Also, under the laws of Descent and Distribution community property will not pass to parents, brothers, sisters or other relatives of the deceased.

SEPARATE PROPERTY

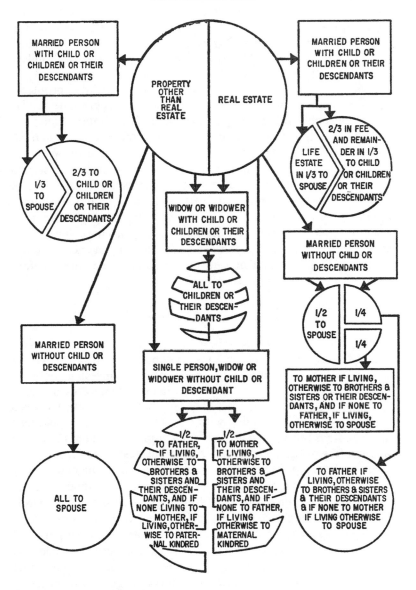

**Figure 9-2.** Separate property distribution without a will.

If a father owning separate property dies without a will, the wife will receive only one-third of the personal property and a life estate in one-third of the real property. This is hardly the disposition the owner of a modest or medium-size estate wants in order to protect the best interest of his wife and children. Yet, this is his will, unless he does something about it.

When a parent is survived by minor children, the problems presented by dying without a will are particularly acute. The surviving spouse is obligated to support the children, and often is required to do so out of his or her own property and earnings, even though the children may have substantial inheritances of their own. Where a minor receives property through inheritance, it is often necessary to have a guardian or a custodian appointed (under the Texas Uniform Gifts to Minors) to protect the property and minor's rights. Insurance companies may require a guardianship or custodianship before they will pay funds to a minor beneficiary. Where a minor inherits an interest in real estate, title companies and lending agencies require that a guardianship be taken out, or a custodian appointed, before the minor's interest can be sold.

### Guardianship—Penalty of Dying Without a Will

The administration of the minor's property under a guardianship is highly restricted and subject to court supervision to safeguard the minor's rights. The minor's money can be invested only in authorized investments, and the guardian's expenditures are also regulated. Although the expenses and restrictions of a court-supervised guardianship may be avoided with a custodianship, both guardians and custodians must deliver the minor's property to the minor at age 18 regardless of the minor's maturity or business experience.

One of the unique advantages of making a will is the opportunity for the parent or grandparent to establish a trust to administer the minor's property. Such a trust will avoid the necessity of a guardianship or custodianship, and the maker can prescribe his own rules for the management of the trust funds, how and for what purposes the money is to be spent, and who is to be the trustee. In addition the trust can continue beyond the time the child comes of age so that he can mature and gain experience in the management of property before it is distributed to him. Further, the final distribution need not be all at once but can be made in installments, enabling the child to assume the responsibility in stages.

### Dying Without a Will—Who Handles the Estate

If an executor is to handle the administration of the decedent's estate but is not named in a will, Texas law provides a list of persons with priorities from which the court will select one individual. The duties of the personal representative (called "executor" if named in the will and "administrator" if appointed by the court) are to locate all of the property of the decedent; manage it during the period of administration; pay all debts, taxes, and costs of administration; and distribute what is left according to the will or the laws of Descent and Distribution. An administrator may or may not be the person the decedent would have selected for the job. It does not have to be the surviving spouse or even a member of the decedent's family and it might even be a creditor. By making a will, the maker can choose the person he feels is best qualified to do the job.

### Each Spouse Should Have a Will

It is important for each spouse to have a will. Since most property owned by married people in Texas is community property, one spouse usually owns half the family wealth. Where there is no will, children automatically inherit the mother's interest in property just as they do the father's. The father may suddenly find himself in partnership with his children in his business as well as the home, car, and all other community property. If the children are minors, the children acting through their guardian or custodian will be the father's new partners. Of course, the father may also be the guardian or custodian, but the guardianship or custodianship could cause financial difficulties if the father is engaged in a business that was acquired as community property. In this case one will alone does only half the job of planning for the family.

### Dying with an Out-Dated Will

Texas law makes special provision for children born or adopted after the execution of a will by their parent. If the surviving spouse is the principal beneficiary under the will and is the parent of all of the decedent's children (other than adopted children), it makes no difference whether a child is born before or after the will was made: the surviving spouse takes the property as provided in the will.

But, if the surviving spouse is not the parent of all of the decedent's children or is not the principal beneficiary, it makes a big difference when a child is born. If there were other children born before the will was made, the child born after the will gets a share of the estate from the beneficiaries. In such a case, the other children get a much smaller share of the estate. In fact, they may get nothing, if they were not originally named as beneficiaries in the will.

In the case that there were no children born before the will was made, a child born after the will may make the will void for practical purposes. The property would then be distributed according to the laws of Descent and Distribution.

## *Divorce—Its Effect on a Will*

A divorce by the maker of a will also affects the provisions of the will. It automatically eliminates from the will of each divorced spouse all provisions affecting the other spouse. As an example, suppose a man makes a will leaving a portion of his estate to his wife. Then, the man and wife are divorced, and the man dies before updating his will. The portion of the estate he designated to go to the wife will not pass to her. Rather, this portion will be distributed to the contingent beneficiaries who would have received the property under the will if the ex-spouse had predeceased the maker. The remainder of the estate will be distributed according to the provisions of the will.

## *Everyone Should Have an Up-to-Date Will*

Even though a person has a properly drawn will that is kept in a place where it can be found at his death, it will be of little value to the beneficiaries if it is not up-to-date. Parenthood, grandparenthood, divorce, changing needs of beneficiaries, change of residence, sale or other disposal of property mentioned in the will, unavailability of an executor or trustee, gifts, newly acquired assets, and a change in the size of the estate are all indications that the will needs to be reviewed by the maker's lawyer. An out-of-date will that no longer fits the maker's desires or the needs of the beneficiaries is little better than no will at all.

Dying without a will rarely, if ever, provides a satisfactory substitute for the making of a will. Without a will a person has no choice as to who will administer his estate, who will be the guardian or custodian of the estate of minor children, or who will receive the property, in what proportions, and when. A will assures the maker that his property goes to the persons he wants it to and in the manner he desires. He can name an executor of his estate, a guardian, a custodian, or a trustee. A will also allows the maker to choose the sources from which debts, expenses of administration, and taxes are to be paid. Further, it can save money in court costs, guardian's fees, and attorney's fees. But even more important are the savings to the family in time, worry, and court appearances and the assurance to them that the maker planned for their continued well-being. A will, very often, is the most important legal document that a property owner executes during his lifetime. It, therefore, deserves thoughtful consideration and skillful preparation.

## *Summary*

A carefully prepared will containing all of the provisions necessary to transmit property from the testator to those he wants to receive it can be a real legacy in itself. Such a will relieves the surviving family of the many problems created by a will improperly prepared or no will at all. It seems, then, that each thoughtful man and woman owes a duty to his family to have a carefully prepared will in keeping with present family circumstances.

# 10

# What Should My Will Contain?

A well-drafted will is tailored to the individual needs and circumstances of the person who signs it, who is called the "testator." An ideal provision in the will of one person might be unfit, and even dangerous, if used in the will of another. Nevertheless, there are numerous provisions that are included in most wills, as well as various problems that should be considered in the drafting of any will.

## Statement of Residence

A will should set forth the county and state of residence of the testator.

## Appointment of an Executor

An executor is a person or corporation who, after the death of a testator, carries out the instructions in a will, pays the debts, and protects and manages the property until it can be delivered to the beneficiaries. A will may appoint a single executor or designate two or more persons or corporations to serve jointly as co-executors. The executor does not have to live in Texas to be eligible to serve. If the will does not appoint an executor, all of the beneficiaries under the will may, with the approval of the probate court, jointly designate a person to serve as executor, or the court will select someone to serve as executor. To avoid the costs of a court appointment and insure that the property will be handled by someone the testator trusts, the testator should appoint an executor in his will. It is also desirable that the will name one or more alternate executors in case the person first named as executor or alternate executor is unable or unwilling to serve.

Unless the will stipulates otherwise, the probate court will require that the person named as executor furnish a bond to guarantee the faithful performance of his duties. The cost of such a bond will be paid out of the testator's estate. Consequently, a testator who desires to avoid this cost should specify in the will that the executor need not give bond. Consideration should also be given to the matter of the executor's compensation for his services. The will should clearly state whether the executor is to serve without compensation or is to be paid some specific amount or in some particular manner.

### *Provision for Independent Administration*

As discussed in Chapter 13, Texans enjoy the advantages of a procedure known as "independent administration," which greatly reduces the costs and delays in handling an estate. However, to insure these advantages, the will should specifically state that the estate is to be given an independent administration. Except in very unusual situations, the will of a Texas resident should always contain this provision.

Another relatively recent development is the statutory independent administration of an estate, available even when the decedent had no will or failed to provide for an independent executor. Since local practice varies as to the availability of this procedure, it is best not to rely on anything but a carefully prepared provision in the will.

### *Provision for Payment of Debts and Taxes*

Even if a will does not contain instructions to pay debts and taxes of the testator, an executor has a general duty to do so. Nevertheless, wills ordinarily contain such instructions, and there is value in this because the testator can spell out his exact wishes about debts and taxes. If, for example, the testator is making installment mortgage payments on his home, he may wish to have his executor pay off the mortgage in full upon his death, or he may want the executor, and thereafter his spouse or some other beneficiary, to continue the installment payments. If continuing the installment payments is desired, the will should say so.

Regarding tax payments, the testator may intend that certain property shall be inherited tax free with the taxes paid out of other property in the estate, or he may want the person receiving the property to pay the death taxes on it. A will should address this issue, rather than leaving it for the executor or the courts to determine.

As discussed in Chapters 5 and 6, the basic Texas inheritance tax has been repealed for heirs of those persons dying on or after September 1, 1981. The amount exempt from federal estate taxation has been increased so that it may be possible for up to $600,000 to pass free of any death taxes. While these changes are quite significant, it does not eliminate the need to consider the proper source of payment of death taxes for larger estates.

### Provisions Disposing of the Property

The principal provisions in most wills are those which set forth to whom and in what manner the testator's property shall pass upon his death. In some states the law requires that a person leave a specified proportion of his property to certain close relatives, and the courts will give such property to the relatives even if the will does not so provide. Texas does not have that requirement. In this state a testator may leave his property to anyone—relative or not—for a good reason, a bad reason, or no reason at all.

Likewise, a testator has great freedom of choice in determining *how* his property shall go to the persons named in his will. He can give the property outright; he can put the property in a trust; or he can give the property on condition that the person receiving it do, or refrain from doing, whatever the testator specifies. Similarly, he can provide that the person receiving the property is to enjoy it only during his lifetime (or for a certain period of time), and that thereafter the property will go to another.

There are certain technical restrictions upon a testator's power to dispose of his property by will. For example, he must not try to control the property for too long, and he must not direct that it be used for an unlawful purpose or for a purpose that violates so-called "public policy." However, subject only to such restrictions, a testator can and should have his will written so that his property will be disposed of in the exact manner he desires. The aim of the lawyer who writes the will should be to find out what the testator wants to do with his property and then to word the will so that it carries out those desires as fully as possible, keeping in mind tax consequences.

Because a testator has such wide latitude in determining how the provisions of his will are to be written, only a few general comments need to be made about them. First and foremost, the will should be written so that it covers *all* of the testator's property. If this is not done, costly court proceedings may be necessary regarding the omitted property. To guard against an omission, a will should always contain a catch-all provision which provides that all property of every kind that has not been disposed of by other portions of the will shall go in a specified manner.

If a testator is putting his property into a trust, or is otherwise tying up its future use and enjoyment, he should be sure to consider whether he wants his home, its furnishings, his automobile, and his personal effects to be included with the other property, or whether he wants his spouse or some other beneficiary to have free and unrestricted ownership of those properties.

The pattern of many wills is to direct that specific pieces of property or sums of money shall go to certain persons, and then to follow up these specific bequests with a general bequest in which the rest of the property is left to others. Thus, a testator may give a shotgun to a friend, a sum of money to a faithful employee or charity, a farm to a certain relative, and so on, with those portions of the will being followed up by a general provision giving the rest of his property to his spouse or children.

Usually the persons who are to receive the rest of the property are the ones whom the testator is most interested in benefiting. A common danger in this type of will is that circumstances may change between the time the will is signed and the time the testator dies. As a result the will may do exactly the opposite of what the testator intended and deny benefits to the very persons whom he wished most to benefit. For example, say a testator had property worth $100,000 in 1982, when he made his will. He wanted his spouse and children to receive the biggest part of his estate, so he worded his will so that five friends or relatives will each receive $5,000, with the rest of the estate going to his spouse and children. However, if his estate has shrunk to $25,000 by the time he dies, the $5,000 bequests will use up the entire estate and, even though the testator intended for his spouse and children to receive most of his property, they will get nothing.

Consequently, whenever a testator is thinking about making specific bequests and then leaving the bulk of his estate to those dearest to him, he should always keep in mind that a decline in the value of his estate may result in its being used up by the specific bequests. One way to prevent this is to make the specific bequests in terms of fractional parts of the estate rather than in terms of dollars and cents. Thus, in the example previously cited, the testator with an original estate of $100,000 should have made the five specific bequests by giving each person 1/20 of his estate, instead of giving $5,000 to each. Then, when the estate had shrunk to $25,000 the five specific bequests would require only $6,250 of the estate, leaving $18,750 for the spouse and children.

## Provision for Alternate Disposition of the Property

When a testator provides in his will that most of his property shall go to a certain person, it ordinarily is wise for him also to provide for a secondary beneficiary in the event that the first person dies before the will takes effect. Many people want to make a chain of alternatives by providing the property shall go to "A, but if he is dead, then to Mrs. A, but if she is dead, then to B," and so on. While it is not practical to provide a long chain of alternative dispositions, it is advisable to have a final beneficiary that will certainly exist at the testator's death, whether a group of persons ("my heirs at law") or an entity such as a charity.

## Provision for Common Accident or Successive Deaths

It is not unusual for a husband and wife to be killed as the result of a common accident or under circumstances that make it difficult to determine who died first. Because the husband's will usually provides for the wife to take some or all of his property, and vice versa, this type of accident can lead to serious problems.

Suppose a husband's will leaves all his property to his wife, with an alternate gift to his parents in the event that she dies before he does, and the wife has left all of her property to the husband, with an alternate gift to her parents. Then, in a common accident the husband dies first and the wife dies a week later. Immediately upon the husband's death, title to his property will go to his wife; and a week later, when the wife dies, title to the property will go to her parents, eliminating his family entirely. Such a double passage of title within a week could result in the imposition of unnecessary death taxes.

Some lawyers use a clause requiring each beneficiary to survive by a specified period of time such as 30 days, or longer. A relatively recent amendment to the Texas Probate Code requires a beneficiary to survive by 120 hours in order to inherit property. This amendment can be overridden by a specific provision in a will.

Other problems can arise if a husband and wife have wills of this kind, and both die from the same accident but it is not known with certainty who died first. The husband's parents may claim the property by asserting that the wife died first, with the wife's parents arguing the contrary. An expensive lawsuit may be required to settle the dispute. Also, the state and federal governments might assert a claim for two sets of taxes by contending that the deaths were not simultaneous. For example, they might take the same position as the wife's parents. The problems resulting from deaths in such circumstances apply not only to spouses but to the deaths of the testator and any beneficiary.

To avoid these problems, every will should contain a clause to deal with this situation. If death results from a common accident, under circumstances that make it difficult to determine whether the testator or the beneficiary died first, or if the deaths occurred within a designated time of each other, such as within 60 or 90 days, the clause should provide for the property to be disposed of as if the testator had died after the beneficiary. Under such a clause there is only one passage of title, and the estate tax and inheritance tax, if applicable, can be imposed only once. The possibility of dual claims to the property is also eliminated.

## Powers for the Executor

So that he can administer the estate with the least amount of time, trouble, and expense, the executor should be given broad powers. Special wording should be used in the will to provide those powers. If the will does not contain such stipulations, the executor is without the necessary powers, and the performance of his duties is made more difficult.

## Provision for Guardianship

When the testator has minor children, the will should appoint a guardian of the person for his children to serve should the other parent die before the will takes effect or should the other parent fail or cease to serve as guardian. A child over 14 years of age may select his own guardian, subject to court approval. But for the guidance of the court, it is wise to name a guardian in the will, even if a child is over 14.

## Contingent Management Provision

A minor child or incompetent person does not have the legal capacity to manage his own property. Generally, the parent of a minor child cannot legally manage the minor's property for him without court proceedings, probably a guardianship for the property, which can be cumbersome and expensive. For this reason provisions should be made in the will to avoid the need for creation of a guardianship for any property passing under the will to a minor child or incompetent person. The will may create a trust for minor children or incompetents, or the will may provide that property that any minor child would otherwise take outright will pass to a custodian for the minor under the Texas Uniform Gifts to Minors Act. The executor of the estate can then appoint the guardian of the person of the minor or an adult member of the minor's family to serve as the custodian to manage the minor's property until he reaches the age of majority.

## Required Formalities

A will must, of course, be signed by the testator. Unless it is entirely written and signed in his own handwriting, it must be signed by at least two witnesses older than the age of fourteen. A beneficiary named in the will should not sign the will as a witness. In the usual will the signature of the testator is followed by a clause reciting that he declared the instrument to be his will, and that the two witnesses have signed the will at his request, in his presence, and in the presence of each other. This clause is then followed by the signatures of the witnesses.

### *"Self-Proved" Will*

The cost and inconvenience of probating the will ordinarily can be reduced if the testator and the witnesses make the will "self-proved" by each signing an acknowledgment and affidavit before a notary public. Having a will self-proven normally means that the witnesses need not appear at the hearing to admit the will to probate. However, self-proving a will is not required, and a will is perfectly valid even if it is not signed before a notary public if it is signed by the required number of witnesses.

### *Summary*

In Texas, a testator has an almost unlimited freedom in determining to whom and how his property shall go upon his death. His will should be "tailor-made" to carry out his wishes and meet the individual needs and circumstances of his estate. However, unless certain formalities are observed and certain common problems are considered, the desires of the testator may be frustrated; the beneficiaries named in his will may get nothing or may receive an estate greatly decreased by unnecessary and costly administrative expenses, death taxes, income taxes, and litigation. In addition to containing carefully drawn provisions disposing of the testator's property, a will should, at the very least, name an executor, grant him broad powers, provide for independent administration, name a guardian of the person for minor children and create a trust for incompetents or minors or direct that a custodian manage the property a minor will inherit, take account of long-term debts, contain a common disaster clause, be properly signed and witnessed, and have a "self-proved" affidavit appended to it.

# 11

# Pitfalls in a Homemade Will

It is known among lawyers that testators who make their own wills often create disputes that only costly litigation can settle. A testator who decides to make his own will no doubt thinks he is saving the fee for preparing the will. Perhaps his philosophy is like that embodied in the following instrument:

"Terrell Tex Jan 12—1950

"this Letter is Written With the idea that Some thing might happen to me. that I would be wiped out Suddenly if this Should Happen my business would be in awful shape no relatives, nobody to do a thing So, this is written to have my affairs wound up in a reasonable way in case of my Sudden Death. Would Like to have all of my affairs, Cash all assets including any Bank Balance turned over to Parties named below With out any Bond or any Court action that can be avoided. they to wind up my affairs in any way they See fit.
U. C. Boyles Refrigeration Supply Co.
Charlie Hill Superior Ice Co
Should these Gentleman need a third man Would Suggest Walker. National Bank of Commerce Each of these Gentleman to receive $500.000 for his Services
I have tried to make my wishes plain. of Course these Crooked Lawyers Would want a Lot of Whereas and Wherefores included in this.
not much in favor of the organized Charities they are too Cold blooded also not much in Favor of any person over 21—Benefitting by

my Kick off unless there is a good reason
am inclined to play the children they are not Responsible for being
here and cant help themselves

"Terrell—Feb. 7—1950

have Let this Letter get cold and Read it again—to See if it Seemed
abut Right
dont See much wrong except no wheres and Wherefores—excuse me

Lon Gresham"

The testator would turn over in his grave if he knew that the instrument in which he had tried to make his "wishes plain" required two trips to the Supreme Court of Texas and excursions through several lower courts to fathom its meaning and consequences.

It is easy to laugh about some of the obvious problems in a will such as Gresham's, but many times learned people make errors just as costly when they draw their own will without legal counsel.

### Is It a Valid Will?

One of the problems involved in the Gresham will was determining whether it was a will. If you read it carefully enough, you might begin to wonder if any property was actually disposed of and if it appointed executors. The courts were divided on whether the instrument was a will. Ultimately the Supreme Court of Texas held that the instrument was a will which disposed of no property but appointed executors to administer the estate.

Often testators leave letters (sometimes even on the back of a match folder) expressing a thought that something should be done upon their deaths. The courts may have difficulty deciding whether such a writing was intended to be the author's last will and testament or was simply the expression of a wish or hope. Following is an example of such an expression which was probated as a will.

"May 25, 1958

In case of death all cash and propity in Tex. go's to Alice. the balance of propity all my airs. Gen. Gavine, Richard, Dalene. Alice also get car and Household goods. Richard also gets the machinery.

Bert Wieneke"

## The Holographic Will

There are two kinds of wills which the layman may attempt to make for himself. One, a "holographic" will, is wholly in the maker's handwriting and is valid in Texas (contrary to the law of other states). The other is one that is typed or otherwise not wholly in the handwriting of the testator. Such an instrument must be executed in accordance with certain prescribed legal requirements or it is void. If a purported will is partly handwritten and partly typed, it is valid only if properly signed and witnessed.

## Was It Properly Executed?

One of the dangers of a will written without professional advice is that the maker may not give sufficient attention to the legal requirements for a valid execution of a will. If these requirements are not followed, the writing cannot be admitted to probate as a will. In Texas there must be at least two witnesses to a non-holographic will who are "credible" and above the age of 14, and who must subscribe their names on the will in their own handwriting, in the presence of the testator after the testator has signed the will.

Texas is unique in providing what is called a "self-proving" affidavit to expedite proof of proper execution of a will when it is offered for probate. The use of such an affidavit is voluntary. If it is used, it must be properly signed and sworn to by the testator and the witnesses before a notary public or other authorized official at the time of execution of the will or later while the testator and the witnesses are still alive. The form of the affidavit is prescribed in the Texas Probate Code.

A self-proved will may be admitted to probate without the testimony of the subscribing witnesses (who may have left the country), and no further proof is necessary.

## Where Is the Will; Are the Witnesses Available?

One of the reasons for executing a will in a lawyer's office is that he provides witnesses who will be available for testimony at a later date when they are needed. He will complete a copy of the will by filling in the date, names of the testator and witnesses and will retain it in his office to evidence the contents of the original will itself as a safeguard should it be lost or destroyed.

### Does It Increase Administration Costs?

Texas is very fortunate in having a form of administration known as the independent administration. Such administration can be conducted by an independent executor named in a will completely free of court control (after the probate of the will and the filing of an inventory, appraisement, and list of claims of the decedent's estate). The advantages of such administration may not be had, however, if the proper words calling for such administration are not stipulated in the will. Homemade wills seldom contain the proper wording.

A testator making his own will may also forget to waive the requirement of bond for the executor, even though it would be his intention to do so. Without a provision for independent executorship and waiver of bond, the probate court might require a bond for a non-corporate executor or administrator. Similarly, one making his own will may fail to waive the bond of a guardian or a trustee for his minor child.

### Is It Clear?

One of the great problems involved in a do-it-yourself will is ambiguity. The central question is: what did the testator really intend? The court must decide.

### Everything to the Wife—What's Left to the Children

An expression which is sometimes found in a will written without legal advice is: "I give my wife everything I have, and upon her death I give what is left for the benefit of my children." Problems are created by such phrasing. Does the wife get the property, or only the right to use it for life? May she sell, mortgage, or lease the property, and if so, how may she invest the proceeds of sale? What happens if the wife mingles the husband's property with her own (including what she may acquire after his death)? Can she give the property away during her lifetime? Ordinarily, the words "for the benefit of" create a trust. Is a trust created for the children? If a trust is created, who is the trustee, and what are the terms of the trust? When does the trust come to an end? These are merely some of the questions raised by such wording.

### Gift of Money; Gift of Land

If a testator states, "I give $25,000 to my three sons," does he mean $25,000 to be divided among the three sons, or does he mean $25,000 to each? If he declares "I give all my land in Dallas County to my son," and the land is subject to a mortgage, does the son have to pay the mortgage or is it paid by the estate?

### "Money on Deposit in Bank"

Another type of ambiguity is that involved in a gift of money on deposit in a bank. Does the statement "I leave the money on deposit at the Fourth National Bank" mean only what was on hand when the will was made (say $1,000) or when the decedent died (say $25,000). And if it turns out that at his death there are two bank accounts, a checking account he had when he made his will and a savings account he opened later, who gets what?

### Gifts of Shares of Stock

Suppose a testator gives $1,000 or ten shares of XYZ stock to Henry Smith. What does the executor do if the XYZ stock is worth $500 a share ($5,000)? Does the beneficiary have his choice?

Another recurring problem is the gift of a specific number of shares of stock without reference to stock splits or stock dividends. For example, the testator may give 100 shares of XYZ stock. Later, a stock dividend of five shares for each one of the original 100 shares is declared. If the provision is interpreted literally, the recipient of 100 shares would have only a fifth the number of shares which the testator may have intended.

### Gift of a Business Interest

Consider the following statement: "I give my business to my son." What happens to the accounts receivables, the inventories, the cash in the bank and other assets belonging to the business? What if the business is located on a piece of land owned by the testator; who gets the land?

## Is It Tailored to the Testator's Needs?

One of the real advantages of obtaining professional advice about what to put in a will is that such discussion helps the testator decide what his basic desires are, what he wishes to do with his property, and what alternatives are available to him to achieve his objectives. Thus, he will more carefully consider the nature and extent of all his assets, the possible ways in which he can aid his family, friends, business associates, and charitable interests. He may be made aware of possibilities that he had never considered before.

For example, if he merely wills his property to his wife or to his children, he may fail to provide properly for the continuation of a business or the handling of a partnership interest, or in some other way handicap his surviving business associates. All of these things can be specifically handled in the will or otherwise during his lifetime in a way that combines the greatest amount of benefit for his family with the least amount of disruption by his death. Often such matters are overlooked by a person making his own will or complicated by incomplete or ambiguous dispositions.

## Does It Unintentionally Disinherit Family Members and Others?

If a testator prepares his own will, he may fail to provide for certain persons he actually wants to benefit. For example, he may leave his property to his only son, or, if the son is not living at the testator's death, to his son's children. The latter event may in fact occur, and his daughter-in-law will get nothing. However she must raise the minor children who will get all the inheritance, and she must do it under the restrictions of a court-supervised guardianship which will continue until the children become 18 years old. Such a guardianship would require the added expense of applications to and orders from the court to do various things in connection with the estate. It would further require the filing and court approval of annual accountings, as well as a final accounting when each child reaches age 18.

Children of a prior marriage may be disinherited inadvertently. An outright gift to a surviving spouse followed by the death of that spouse would result in the surviving spouse's children getting the entire inheritance, while the children of the prior marriage would be disinherited.

Sometimes a testator writing his own will makes large bequests of money to friends or others. Such incidental bequests may leave little for the real object of his beneficense due to a shrinkage in his estate or because of a failure to account for estate liabilities.

A family member may be disinherited inadvertently from a gift under the will by being asked to witness the will. Although there are several protective features in the law to cover such a situation, if a witness is required to testify in order to probate the will, he must give up the gift, unless he would have inherited the same property under the laws of intestacy.

### *Does It Make Administration More Difficult?*

Serious problems can arise with respect to the powers of executors if the powers are not provided for carefully. Many times such powers and the method of administering the property are overlooked by testators who make their own wills. In Texas one of the most serious administrative commissions would be the failure to provide for an independent executor without bond and with power of sale.

### *Does It Make Other Significant Omissions?*

Many other important matters are often overlooked in the self-made will. There may be a failure to give directions to an executor as to what to do about taxes due on a life insurance policy. The estate without the insurance may be non-taxable, but the large insurance policy could cause the estate to have to pay an estate tax. Who should pay the tax on the insurance proceeds—the individual named in the policy, or the persons entitled to the residue of the estate under the will?

The self-made will may fail to designate a successor executor or trustee in the event the original named executors or trustee fails to serve or dies. This would be particularly unfortunate if it were a named independent executor. In the absence of the designation of a successor, the administration would have to proceed with an administrator under court control.

Sufficient attention may not be given to the possibility of one death occurring within a short time of another. If a testator gives all his property to a surviving wife, all the property may go to her family to the complete exclusion of his family, even though there may be only a few minutes difference in the times of their deaths.

## Summary

There are many reasons why it is not advisable for a person inexperienced in legal terms and consequences to attempt to execute his own will. Such wills constitute a prolific source of litigation with resulting family disputes and greatly increased costs of probate.

This poem by Lord Neaves is dedicated to those seeking to avoid the lawyers fee for preparing a will:

Ye lawyers who live upon litigants' fees,
And who need a good many to live at your ease,
Grave or gay, wise or witty, whate'er you decree,
Plain stuff or Queen's Counsel, take counsel of me.
When a festive occasion your spirit unbends,
You should never forget the Profession's best friends;
So we'll send round the wine and bright bumper fill,
To the jolly testator who makes his own will.

# 12
# Choosing the Right Executor

Selecting the right executor is one of the testator's most important decisions. The one appointed will be the decedent's agent to carry out the wishes and desires expressed in his will. Integrity, business experience, impartiality, willingness to serve, and sound judgment should be taken into consideration when selecting an executor.

In our complex society it is not often possible to find any one person with the time, experience, and qualifications of the ideal executor. Frequently, services are obtained from a variety of sources such as the surviving spouse, lawyer, accountant, business partner, close family friend, and other family members.

One of the most difficult jobs for any executor is to identify the assets of the estate and locate the appropriate records relating to them. This task is most easily done by a surviving spouse or adult child. When these records are made available to a competent lawyer, much of the detail work can be accomplished under the lawyer's direction—either by the client or by a member of the lawyer's staff. The desire to be involved frequently helps a bereaved family member to adjust to the fact of death and obtain familiarity with the estate of the decedent. Thus, this opportunity is extremely valuable and should not be overlooked.

## Duties and Powers

The executor's goal is to handle the estate in the very best interests of the persons who will inherit it. The executor should preserve and manage the estate and see to the payment of obligations. He should treat the assets of the estate fairly, impartially, and confidentially.

The powers given to an executor in a will may be limited to paying debts, expenses, and taxes. Or, they may be broad and include the rights of disposing of property, making a division among the devisees, and operating a business. An executorship may be continued for many years or may be limited to a short period of time.

Certain actions are necessary in any estate where there is a will naming an executor. Within a reasonable time after the testator's death, the will should be taken to the attorney representing the estate who will file an application for its probate. At that time the executor should know generally the nature and extent of the properties of the estate. After the application is filed and proper notice is given, a court hearing is held in order to prove the will and admit it to probate and record. The executor then qualifies and secures authority from the court to act.

He is responsible for ascertaining the properties left by the testator, as well as his debts and obligations. He must prepare a list of the properties to be submitted to appraisers appointed by the court. If there is a going business he must supervise it. It is most important that the proper insurance be kept in force on properties, and that any rights the estate might have be kept intact. After debts have been paid—including whatever taxes are due—the executor gives his final accounting and makes distributions to the devisees as directed under the will.

Who, then, should be chosen as the right executor?

## The Surviving Spouse

The surviving spouse may be capable of assuming the responsibilities of the estate. Frequently, however, a widow (or even a widower) is untrained in the business of probate and tax problems involved. Under such circumstances it may be better to appoint a bank, a partner, another member of the family, or a trusted friend as executor. Eventually, the surviving wife will be expected to manage her own affairs but this can be done gradually as she acquires some knowledge of the problems involved. Perhaps a co-executorship is the answer. The surviving spouse can act together with the steadying hand of one more experienced.

*A Bank*

Many banks have been granted trust powers. Their trust departments are strictly supervised by state and federal authorities. As executor, a bank may employ an attorney and an accountant in handling the estate. Instructions may be left, however, either in the will, or separately, which specify an attorney and an accountant.

The executor will be entitled to charge those fees allowable by law in Texas. The law (Section 241 of the Probate Code) provides that an executor shall be entitled to receive a commission of 5 percent on sums he receives in cash and 5 percent on sums he pays out in cash in the administration of the estate. No commission is allowed for receiving cash belonging to the deceased and which is on hand or on deposit in a bank. Nor is a commission allowed for paying out cash to the heirs or legatees. An individual, such as the surviving spouse, a child, or a trusted friend, although entitled to charge the same fee as any executor, may serve the estate and charge little, if anything, other than actual expenses incurred.

*An Alternate Executor*

An executor must, of course, live longer than the person appointing him. It is good, therefore, not to name someone more advanced in age than the testator. The vicissitudes of life are such that an alternate, or successor, executor should be appointed in every will, with the same powers and rights as the first executor named.

As noted in the preceeding chapter, it is not wise to attempt to draw one's own will. There are numerous pitfalls which may make that attempt to save money most expensive to the estate. This includes appointing an executor without proper expressions concerning his powers and responsibilities.

An attorney can prepare the will so that a minimum of court supervision is necessary. Continuous probate court supervision of the actions of the executor or administrator may involve heavy and unnecessary expense. In Texas the executor can be made independent of the court and authorized to serve without bond. If such independence and service without bond is not expressed in the will, the probate court will not only require a bond (except in the case of a bank), but it will be necessary for the executor to make separate applications to the court for authority to act in behalf of the estate in all matters. These applications are not only time consuming but costly and annoying.

### Co-Executors

The problem of choosing the right executor may be solved by appointing two or more persons as co-executors. A testator may not want to name one child over another for fear of the possible friction. This problem may be solved by naming two or more children as joint or co-executors.

It is quite common for a husband and wife to name the survivor as executor. The surviving spouse may be entirely capable of being executor, and as such would act with the utmost in economy to the estate. However, a widow often finds herself at a complete loss when the complex problems of modern business are suddenly thrust upon her. Under such circumstances she might welcome the service of a trusted friend or the trust department of a bank as co-executor. When a bank acts as co-executor, it is customary for it to have physical custody of bonds, securities, and other properties of the estate, subject to the right of the other co-executor to inspect the properties and records at all reasonable times.

An executor cannot act until the will is admitted to probate by the court. There may, however, be certain urgent matters which require attention before the executor can formally qualify. If the deceased was engaged in a going business, it should continue to operate. If there are perishable assets in the estate, they should be protected. It may be necessary to arrange for funds to take care of expenses incidental to the operation of a going business or the decedent's last illness. In choosing your executor you should consider the willingness and ability of the person or institution named to take over the above matters before formal qualification as executor.

### Telling Your Executor

An executor should be consulted before being appointed and named in a will to determine whether he is willing to act. After the will is prepared, it is a good practice to furnish the executor with a copy and to tell him where the original will is to be located for safekeeping.

Consider the case of John and Mary Doe. They were a married couple with three small children. John and Mary had separate wills, but in each provision was made that if they should die in a common disaster, or within a short time of one another, their estates were to be handled by an executor and trustee for the benefit of the children. The contingency happened, but neither John nor Mary had advised the executor of his appointment or of the location of their wills. Administration proceedings on the estates were initiated under the mistaken belief that wills did not exist.

Eventually the wills were found, and the executor named offered them for probate and qualified as executor. The administration taken out before the wills were discovered was closed, and the properties of the estate were handed over to the qualified executor. Extra time and expense could have been avoided had John and Mary Doe advised their executor that they had made wills and the location of them.

## Attributes of an Executor

Consideration in choosing the executor are much the same as would be given to choosing a business partner. The necessary attributes may be summarized as follows:

*Integrity.* An executor should have the ultimate interests of the heirs in mind at all times. This requires soundness of moral principal and character. He must be unselfish and honest in all dealings with the estate.

*Business ability.* Sound business judgment, combined with actual experience, is a desired quality. Many economies result from experience, and the testator's ultimate aim is to see that as much of the estate as possible passes to the beneficiaries named in the will.

*Executorship ability.* The handling of an estate requires knowledge of the rights and responsibility of an executor, and the ability to carry them out. With larger estates, knowledge of income taxation, as well as estate and inheritance taxes, is necessary.

*Availability.* The time a person has to devote to the handling of the estate depends on its size and complexity. If an executor is to keep the best interests of the beneficiaries in mind, he must have the time to devote to the executorship. In handling large estates, the duties may be so time-consuming that an individual executor would have to neglect his personal business interests. In such a case a trust institution should be selected since it has officers and employees specially trained in handling estate matters.

*Impartiality.* Whether the executor is the surviving spouse, child, friend, or trust institution, complete impartiality must be given to all heirs under the will. Such impartiality may be impossible from a member of the family. If the testator fears lack of impartiality, he should consider someone outside of the family.

*Discretion.* Handling an estate may bring an executor into contact with family problems which neither the testator nor his survivors want publicly aired. It is therefore important that the executor be a person who will conduct estate matters confidentially. It is his privilege to serve the deceased, and it is the right of the testator to expect matters held in confidence during his lifetime to be so maintained after his death.

## Summary

A testator intends for the accumulations of a lifetime to be handled prudently. He should, therefore, select an executor who possesses sound business judgment tempered with concern for the heirs and devisees.

In recent years people have given more thought to planning their estates than in the past. This is attributable to the ever growing difficulty in accumulating, managing, and preserving property. Taxation and its adverse effects are of special concern. A will, no matter how simple, should be prepared for every property owner, and it should include an earnest attention to the selection of an executor. An executor, in order to serve the estate in the best possible way must—like the operator of a successful business—have the necessary experience, knowledge, and seasoned judgment, as well as the time to devote to estate affairs.

# 13

# Importance of an Independent Administration

Texas can proudly claim one lasting contribution to American jurisprudence—the concept of an independent administration. An independent administration provides a means for effecting the settlement of a decedent's estate free from the control of the probate court. The formal process whereby a decedent's estate is administered by an executor or administrator, under the supervision of a probate court, is a common law development. Its origin has been attributed to the sovereign's desire to protect creditors and secure the payment of taxes. This judicial supervision of the personal representative forms the basis of the elaborate, present-day systems of estate administration in the United States.

But in 1843 the Seventh Congress of the Republic of Texas gave statutory birth to another type of administration, now commonly termed as "independent administration." It provided for including in a will the directive "that no other action than the probate and registration of this will shall be had in the probate court." This authorized for the first time in America the settlement of a decedent's affairs without judicial supervision. Such right is presently available to Texans under Section 145 of the Texas Probate Code. Without this statutory authorization, a person has no right to keep his estate from the court given jurisdiction to supervise its administration. Until the advent of the Uniform Probate Code, only three other states (Arizona, Idaho, and Washington) permitted independent administration. Now in effect in several states, the

Uniform Probate Code has adopted many of the concepts that have previously been available in Texas through independent administration.

## Purpose of an Independent Administration

This legislation was designed to provide a better and more effective method for settling a decedent's estate with the minimum bother, delay, and cost necessary to probate a will. After probating the will and returning an inventory of the estate, the independent executor/administrator is not required to report to or obtain any authority from the probate court. He is not required to file annual accountings or final accountings.

He is not required to present an application to or obtain authority from the court to make sales or compromise claims. And he is not subject to the direction of the court in any of his other activities in the settlement of the decedent's estate. This freedom is the essence of an independent administration. The popularity of this device and its almost universal utilization by Texas attorneys attests to the admirable way it accomplishes its purpose. It is truly the most significant feature of the Texas probate system.

## How to Obtain an Independent Administration

Prior to the 1977 amendments to the Texas Probate Code, a person had to make a will to obtain the benefits of this extrajudicial administration. These and subsequent amendments to Section 145 of the Texas Probate Code grant to the court the ability to enter an order authorizing independent administration and appointing an independent executor/administrator in each of the following situations:

1. Where an executor is named in a will but the will does not provide for independent administration.
2. Where no executor is named in the will or where each executor named is deceased or disqualified or is unwilling to serve as executor.
3. Where there is no will, that is, an intestate succession.

While all of the heirs and beneficiaries must agree to employ this procedure, Texas has provided additional statutory authorization for the use of independent administrations. Because of the possibility that the heirs or beneficiaries might not agree or that the court might decide that independent administration is not in the best interest of the estate, ample justification for making a will still exists in order to secure the privilege of estate administration free from judicial supervision.

A testator should still indicate in his will if it is his desire to have an independent administration. No magic words are required: any indication that the executor is to be free of the court's control is ample. While use of the term "independent" is not required, Texas courts have held that an independent administration is created when a testator nominates an "independent executor." Although the use of the phraseology of the statute itself is doubtless most common and least likely to be questioned, it is by no means indispensable. The simple statement "I wish my estate kept out of the probate court," has been ruled as adequate by courts in the past.

Again, because of the possibility that the heirs or beneficiaries might not agree or that the court might find that it would not be in the best interest of the estate to grant an independent administration, a testator who wishes to employ the advantages of independent administration should name an independent executor to hold this special trust. A testator may appoint any number of persons, real or corporate, to execute his will. If he does not personally designate one to hold this office, it is possible that the court may do it for him, with the consent of all the heirs or beneficiaries, but in most instances the testator will name an independent executor and one or more alternate independent executors so that some person in whom he has complete trust and confidence will always be available to carry out his wishes.

### What is an Independent Executor/Administrator?

The position of an independent executor/administrator is somewhat unique. "He takes charge of and administers the estate of his testator without action of the county court in relation to the settlement of the estate and may do, without an order, every act which an executor administering an estate under the control of the court may do with such order." He is untrammeled "by orders of the court directing or commanding what he shall do in the management and administration of the estate. He is an executor at large, exercising his own judgment and discretion . . . he is an independent executor."

But an independent executor/administrator is not a law unto himself. He is required to conform to the probate laws so far as they are applicable. His independence consists largely in his right to act without a court order. For example, unless authorized by the will, he cannot sell property for the purpose of reinvesting the proceeds or for other business management reasons. It is, therefore, common to provide in a will that, in addition to the powers conferred by law, the independent executor shall have the powers of a trustee. This insures the independent executor/administrator of the most flexible powers.

To understand the great difference in the independent administration and one subject to court supervision, consider an action required to sell a single town lot to pay debts owed by the decedent. The non-independent administrator would first present an application to the county court requesting authority to sell the town lot. After proper citation had been posted (a period of 10 days), a hearing could be held in which the court might authorize the sale of the lot on terms and conditions specified at the hearing. After making the sale, the administrator would file a report of sale with the court, indicating that a sale had been made under the conditions specified in the earlier court order. This report would remain on file for 5 days. Then the court could after a hearing confirm or reject the sale. Only with the court's confirmation of the sale could the purchaser acquire good title.

An independent executor/administrator would not be involved in any of these delays. He would simply negotiate the best sale he could and convey the property title to the purchaser. Little difference would be discernible between his activities and those of a trustee performing the same task. Indeed an independent administration is often referred to by the courts as a trust. For all practical purposes, the independent executor/administrator stands in the shoes of the decedent whose estate he is administering.

*Enforcement of an Independent Executor's/Administrator's Duties*

The purposes of any administration are to settle the decedent's affairs, to satisfy the claims of the creditors and taxing authorities, and to distribute the remainder of the estate in accordance with the testator's directions. Ample protection is afforded to insure the independent executor's/administrator's faithful performance of such obligations. Provisions are made requiring an independent executor/administrator to post bond as a safeguard against mismanagement. The 1979 amendments to the Texas Probate Code provide for procedures under which interested persons may petition the court for an accounting and distribution of the estate's assets and removal of the independent executor/administrator for failure to file an accounting, misapplication of estate property, misconduct, or incompetency. A creditor may sue the independent executor/administrator directly without securing approval of his claim by a probate court and may use ordinary processes, e.g., attachment, garnishment, or execution, to force the independent executor/administrator into paying the decedent's debts. A creditor may also require those receiving a portion of the estate to post bond or even have the estate settled under the direction of the court.

If the testator does not relieve the independent executor/administrator of the necessity of posting bond, the independent executor/administrator must post an appropriate bond to qualify, just as a dependent executor must. If sound discretion is used in the selection of an independent executor or independent administrator, little justification exists for requiring the estate to incur the additional expense of a bond, and most testators take advantage of this savings opportunity. In the case of an independent executor/administrator appointed by the court under the 1977 amendments to the Texas Probate Code, appropriate bond must be posted in order to qualify, unless the court specifically waives the requirements of such a bond.

### Advantages of an Independent Administration

An independent administration is free from many formalities and delays encumbering an ordinary administration. This makes possible a quicker, less expensive settlement of a decedent's estate, while affording ample protection for creditors and the minimum reporting necessary for tax purposes. The independent administration probably has much to do with the fact that Texas legal fees in probate rank a low thirty-seventh among the other states (*Trusts and Estates*, September, 1966, page 850), although not all administrations in Texas are independent, and the inheritance and estate taxes work the same in Texas as elsewhere.

## Summary

Because of the laws authorizing an independent administration, much of the criticism of the probate process in the United States is inapplicable to Texas. The opportunities for political or legal abuses are largely gone when there is no detailed court supervision.

An independent executor without bond and with general authority from the testator who appoints him can accomplish the least expensive, most effective, and quickest settlement of an estate. An independent executor/administrator appointed by the court, even though he may have to post a bond in order to qualify, can still accomplish basically the same results even in those instances where for some reason an independent executor would not otherwise be available. This added authority was granted to the court and to the beneficiaries in the 1977 amendments to the Texas Probate Code. The great flexibility of an independent administration can make it almost as effective as the decedent himself might have been in managing his property.

# 14

# Will Substitutes—
# Jointly Owned Property

## *Origin*

Many people believe that an ideal method of owning property is "joint tenancy with right of survivorship." Although there are advantages of joint ownership of property, there are several disadvantages which should be carefully considered. Even with the widespread use today of joint tenancies for certificates of deposit and other cash-equivalent investments, the ownership of property with right of survivorship is not a new idea. It was an early common law favorite. If two or more persons bought property and had title taken in both names, the presumption was that they intended to own it with right of survivorship. So, if land was sold to Doe and to Smith, and if neither had sold his interest prior to the death of one, the survivor owned the entire property interest. The reasoning was that when one died, his interest in the tract also died, and the survivor owned all. This was their agreement.

From a practical standpoint, the chief characteristic of joint tenancy is that the survivor owns the entire interest. The appealing aspect of it is the saving of time and expenses in probate by permitting the survivor to own the property automatically. In the early common law in England, the purpose of joint tenancy was to minimize or avoid feudal tenures or duties, the predecessors of present day death taxes.

In time this chief characteristic lost its appeal, partly because of the abolition of the early feudal taxes, and partly because it became less desirable to have the ultimate ownership dependent on chance of survival. The owner of a joint interest could not dispose of it by his will. If he died without a will, his interest would not go to his heirs. If a joint tenant wanted his interest to go at his death to somebody other than his joint tenant, the joint tenancy had to be severed during the lives of the joint tenants. The presumption of feudal times changed during subsequent common law development from that favoring right of survivorship to that favoring a tenancy-in-common ownership. Now, if Jones and Fox bought land together, it was presumed that they owned it as tenants-in-common. Unlike the joint tenancy earlier favored, if Jones died, his interest would pass under his will, and if he died without a will, his interest would go to his heirs; at his death the survivor would not own any more interest than he owned before the death of his co-tenant. The chief characteristic of co-tenancy, then, is that the deceased co-tenant's interest passes as a part of his estate.

It was subsequently the rule that if two persons bought property, as joint tenants with right of survivorship and not as tenants-in-common, (or words of similar meaning showing this intent), the survivor owned the entire interest at the death of the other. It could be seen clearly by their express agreement that they intended for the survivor to take all. But in the absence of this agreement, it was felt that the ultimate ownership of property should not be determined by chance of survival.

Many states have express statutes concerning these early presumptions. The majority of these statutes provide that if parties buy property, it shall not be presumed that they own it with right of survivorship. In most states the right of survivorship is possible, but is must be clearly shown that this was the intention of the owners.

### Origin in Texas

In 1848, the Texas Legislature adopted the forerunner of the present Texas Probate Code, Sec. 46, entitled "Joint Tenancies." Its present version provides that where two or more persons hold an interest in property jointly and one joint owner dies, his interest does not survive to the remaining joint owner but passes by his will or intestacy. By an agreement in writing of joint owners of property, the interest of any joint owner who dies may be made to survive to the surviving joint owner. A survivorship agreement does not result from the mere fact that the property is held in joint ownership, or with an "or" between the names of the co-owners.

Until 1939 there was very little, if any, litigation concerning this statute. In that year a Texas court had before it the effect of a deed to two brothers as joint tenants with right of survivorship. After the death of one of the brothers, the surviving brother mortgaged the entire tract. The question was whether the survivor owned all the tract, or only half the tract. The court held that the purpose of "joint tenancies" statute was not to abolish the power to own property with right of survivorship, but to abolish the early common law presumption that property bought by two or more would be owned with survivorship. It was held that the owners of property, in this case, could expressly provide for survivorship and that, therefore, the surviving brother owned and could mortgage the entire tract.

Shortly after World War II the early common law idea of right of survivorship was rediscovered in Texas. Many thought that this was a completely new idea created to do away with probate. Many misconceptions about joint tenancy and its proper uses came about, and its limitations and disadvantages were often overlooked as a result.

The simplicity of survivorship has always been appealing; this convenient and inexpensive method of passing ownership of property is available today in certain situations under Texas law. Although it is not a fair statement to say that property should never be held in survivorship form, neither is it fair to say that all property should be held in survivorship form in order to save time, money, and possible litigation at an owner's death.

### Problems in Community Property States

Since Texas is a community property state, certain problems have been created here in attempting to adopt the common law form of survivorship in holding and owning community property. Those who have been educated in the common law states (as distinguished from the eight community property states which adopted the Civil Law of Spain or France as the basis of marital property rights), frequently overlook the community property aspect of the problem in their writings and advice to Texas husbands and wives.

It is thought that the bulk of property now held in survivorship form in Texas consists of U.S. Savings Bonds, bank and savings and loan accounts, and securities.

A review of some of the litigation that has reached the Texas courts since 1948 involving disputes between family and non-family members over the ownership of property held in survivorship will best illustrate the advantages and shortcomings of survivorship provisions.

In 1987, the Texas Constitution was amended to make possible, for the first time, creation by a husband and wife of joint tenancies with right of survivorship out of community property. In 1989, the Texas Probate Code was amended to add to Texas law provisions that specify the method of creating these survivorship arrangements. Upon death of a spouse, all property held subject to a valid joint tenancy passes to the surviving spouse independent of the decedent's will. No formal court action is necessary, although a court procedure is available if the survivor wants the certainty of a judicial decree that he or she is the full owner of the property.

## Government Bonds

Frequently U.S. Bonds are registered in two or more names. A common method of registering such bonds is "John Doe or Mary Doe" (husband and wife). A problem often arises if John or Mary Doe dies. Does half the interest in these bonds pass under the decedent's will or belong to the survivor named on the bond? After conflicting court rulings in the several states, including Texas, it was held by the U.S. Supreme Court in 1962 that the survivor named on the bond became the sole owner at the death of the other co-owner. In this test case (which came from Texas), a husband and wife had purchased with community funds bonds which were valued at $87,035.50 when the wife died. In her will, she gave her share of the community property to her son. In a suit between the husband and the son to determine whether the mother's will was effective, the U.S. Supreme Court held that the bonds belonged solely to the surviving husband. The high court held that a Treasury Regulation providing for the survivor becoming the sole owner upon the death of a co-owner was paramount to Texas law. The Texas Supreme Court decision which had given the surviving son half of the value of the bonds was reversed. The U.S. Supreme Court recognized that there is a possibility that a Texas spouse can commit fraud upon the other spouse by placing community funds in an "or" form registration. However, to prove fraud, a suit would be required by the surviving spouse.

The situation where this can arise is shown in a Texas case involving alleged fraud. The husband had purchased $18,000 worth of U.S. Bonds and had registered them in his name and that of a daughter from a prior marriage. Upon his death the daughter claimed the ownership of all the bonds under the U.S. Treasury Regulations. In a suit seeking half value of the bonds, the surviving wife claimed that her husband had used community funds to purchase the bonds, thus converting her share of the community funds to his daughter. The wife failed to prove that community funds were used to buy the bonds, and she lost her case.

When a U.S. Savings Bond is registered in the name of two individuals as co-owners, either may redeem it without permission of the other. Upon the death of one, the surviving co-owner becomes the sole owner. If a bond is registered, "Richard Brown, payable on death to Richard Brown, Jr.," then upon the death of Richard Brown, the named beneficiary becomes the sole owner. The bonds are not a part of the probate estate of the first to die and are not liable for payment of the decedent's debts. However, this form of registration should not be used if the person who furnishes the purchase money wants to leave the bonds to someone in his will other than the registered co-owner.

Contrary to what may be a fairly common belief, there is no estate or inheritance tax savings in using this form of bond registration, nor in owning or holding any kind of property in a survivorship title. If the bonds were purchased with community funds and registered "husband and wife, with rights of survivorship" or "payable to the survivor," half the value will be included for death tax purposes in the taxable estate of the first spouse to die. The surviving spouse, as a named co-owner or survivor, becomes the sole owner of the bonds. The bonds are not a part of the probate estate of the deceased spouse. If the bonds are owned by the surviving spouse at his or her subsequent death, the full amount of the bonds may be subject to federal and state death taxes at the survivor's death and will be a part of the survivor's probate estate. If the owner of property places property in his name and that of another as "joint tenants with right of survivorship" and if the owner dies first, then the survivor may pay federal and state death taxes on the property which the survivor now fully owns. If the amount of the property acquired through the survivorship provision is less than the amount of property sheltered from tax by the available federal estate and gift tax unified credit, then no tax will be due. The fact that no tax is due is because of the amount of property sheltered by the tax credit and not because the property is owned as joint tenants with right of survivorship. The maximum amount of property which can be passed free of federal and state tax is $600,000 unless the owner used all or part of the estate and gift tax credit during lifetime.

A word of caution also is needed about the taxation of the deceased spouse's share of jointly owned bonds, or other property, for federal estate tax purposes. The 1976 Tax Reform Act made several changes in prior federal estate tax laws in the determination of the taxable estate in relation to jointly owned property. Simply stated, the problem is that the federal government is not particularly interested in the identity of the new owner of the property and whether the new owner acquires ownership through will, inheritance, or by survivorship provisions. The primary concern of the federal government is the extent of property to be included within the taxable estate of the decedent. U.S. Treasury regulations do prescribe, however, that a named co-owner will be the sole owner of U.S. government bonds, and this is true, even though the original owner of the funds who purchased the bonds may provide differently in his will. If a person's potential estate exceeds the amount of property sheltered by the federal estate and gift tax credit, the person should obtain current information from an attorney knowledgeable in estate planning concerning the presumptions of ownership, the date of the creation of the joint tenancy property, and whether a taxable gift had been reported at the time of the creation of the joint ownership. The problems will involve whether community or separate property was placed in the survivorship provision, and whether the joint owners are married or not. A father placing separate property in his name and that of his daughter as joint tenants with right of survivorship may pass the entire ownership to the daughter surviving at father's death, but estate tax problems cannot be avoided by such ownership. Since 1982, spouses may under certain conditions pass between them by gift or inheritance an unlimited amount of property, utilizing the unlimited marital deduction provisions of the federal estate tax statutes. By utilizing the provisions of Texas law allowing creation of joint tenancies between spouses using either separate or community property, spouses may thus pass property to each other free of tax using this method or any other method, including outright gifts and transfers by will. However, careful long-range estate planning, the amount of property which can be passed to any person free of tax, and the likelihood of fluctuations in value of any person's assets, strongly suggest that parties obtain current estate-planning advice from an attorney knowledgeable in that field before placing significant amounts of assets in joint tenancies.

### Bank Accounts

Since 1948 most of the lawsuits in Texas concerning survivorship provisions have involved the ownership of money in the bank at the death of one of those authorized to sign checks on a checking or savings account. The decisions indicate failure on the part of many to distinguish and understand the difference between an agency account and a survivorship account. To avoid confusion the term "joint account" should not be used. This is the popular term, but it is misleading. The terms "convenience account" (also called "agency account" or "authorization account") and "survivorship account" should be used to distinguish clearly between the two different type accounts held in the name of two or more in a bank or savings and loan association.

In 1979, the Texas Legislature codified provisions relating to joint accounts, which should help clarify previous uncertainties relating to both survivorship and non-survivorship joint accounts both during lifetime and at the death of one of the owners. However, there will continue to be problems with unintended results from creation of joint accounts because of lack of understanding of consequences of survivorship provisions. Competent legal advice should be sought before creation of joint accounts of significant size in which the joint party may not be the sole intended beneficiary of the owner's estate.

A typical person likely to have a bank account on which two or more are authorized to sign checks is the elderly widow who lives alone. She wants someone to be authorized to sign checks to pay her bills. She authorized someone else—a child, a bookkeeper, a nurse, or the next-door-neighbor—to sign checks on her account. The question that must be determined is whether the owner of the account wants the third person to own the balance. If so, she asks for a signature card, signed by both, which contains the express provision "as joint tenants with right of survivorship and not as tenants in common." This clearly indicates that the elderly widow wants the third party to have the funds in her account at her death. This is a simple substitute for a provision in her will.

However, if the widow wants the third party to sign checks only, she asks for an "authorization," or "agency," or "convenience" card. There is no intent to pass ownership of the balance to the third party. The balance is a part of the widow's estate at her death. The point is that there is nothing objectionable to the widow's giving the balance to the third party friend or relative who is assisting her in her business matters, but the problem comes after the widow's death when the question arises: "Did the widow intend that this friend or relative own what was left in the bank?"

Several Texas cases illustrate this problem. In one a woman who owned a bank account signed a signature card with a third party of no relation to her. The card contained the provision that ". . . the funds are to be owned jointly, with right of survivorship . . . " The woman's will provided that the checking account in this particular bank go to her three brothers. At her death it was held that the third party owned the balance in the account due to the survivorship agreement printed on the card. Another case involved a daughter who was permitted to write checks on her mother's account. At the mother's death the daughter claimed the bank balance as hers because of the survivorship provision in the signature card. In a suit filed by the other sisters, it was proved that the mother had made a mistake in signing this particular card. She had intended a convenience account, not a survivorship account.

Because of a change in the Texas statute, the courts now hold that evidence may not be introduced at trial of a case to prove that the deceased intended a convenience account. Instead, the person designated as the joint tenant with right of survivorship takes the account, regardless of what the deceased intended.

Now, both separate and community property held in spouses' joint names with right of survivorship can be made to pass to the surviving spouse. It has also been held by the Supreme Court that a husband could deposit community funds in his name and that of his daughter (by prior marriage) "or the survivor," and at the death of the father, the daughter became the sole owner of the balance. The decision was based upon the assumption that the father intended the funds as a gift to the daughter. The wife would be required to show fraud by the husband to set aside this disposition of her share of the community funds.

Points relevant to agency bank accounts are also applicable to owning shares of stock and other assets registered in two or more names with right of survivorship.

## *Summary*

Joint ownership of property can reduce the original owner's complete control over the property. Because he is sharing ownership, under law he will also share management and control of the property. There are no tax advantages in owning property in joint tenancy, but there can be tax disadvantages. Many people believe that by placing property in a survivorship form, it will not be subject to a death tax. This is not so. Any assets shown to be owned by a decedent, whether placed in joint tenancy or not, will be subject to estate tax if the value of all assets in an estate exceeds the value of assets sheltered by the federal estate and gift tax credit. This credit will allow tax-free passage of substantial amounts of property. The unlimited marital deduction provisions of the federal estate and gift tax statutes now allow tax-free passage of unlimited amounts of property between spouses. Parties with substantial estates, including jointly owned property, should obtain the advice of an attorney knowledgeable in estate planning before making major plans or changes in the ownership of property or its potential distribution at death.

A survivorship agreement intended to cover all assets may not be a complete substitute for a will. If new assets are acquired, the agreement will not cover them unless amended, and a costly intestacy could result. Assets which should be placed in trust for management or tax planning reasons cannot be properly directed under a survivorship agreement. Before placing property in survivorship form, the owner should clearly understand the effect of sharing ownership of property with another prior to the original owner's death. The owner should keep in mind three areas in which problems have arisen: (1) subsequent ownership and management of the property prior to the death of first to die, (2) liability of jointly owned property for debts of either named co-owner, and (3) taxation by both state and federal governments on jointly owned property. The owner of a bank account should clearly understand the distinction between a "convenience or authorization (agency)" and a "joint tenancy with right of survivorship" account. In the former, the authorized person or agent does not acquire ownership of the balance in the bank account at the death of the owner; in the latter, the survivor does acquire ownership in the balance, and it may not be proved that the deceased owner intended otherwise.

# 15

# Will Substitutes—
# The Revocable Trust

The revocable trust as an instrument in estate planning has been increasingly popular in the past few years. A *trust* is the separation of the ownership of property into two parts with legal title (or management) of the property in one person and beneficial ownership of the property in another person. There are two broad categories of trusts—the living trust and the testamentary trust. A *living trust* is created during the maker's lifetime, while a *testamentary trust* is created upon the maker's death by his will.

Further, there are two classes of living trusts, revocable and irrevocable. A *revocable trust,* as its name implies, is one that can be cancelled or changed during its existence. Withdrawal of all or any part of the trust assets can be made at any time at the request of the maker of the revocable trust. An *irrevocable trust,* then, is one which cannot be altered.

It is also desirable to know the terms used in connection with trusts. The maker of a trust is the *grantor* or *settlor*. The person or bank who is given legal title, possession, and management of the trust assets is the *trustee*. And the person who benefits from the trust is the *beneficiary.*

## Terms of a Typical Revocable Trust

In the typical revocable living trust a grantor transfers property to a trustee under a written agreement. The agreement provides for the trustee to pay the grantor all of the income from the trust during his lifetime, together with such amounts of principal as may be requested by the grantor. It also provides that the grantor can amend or revoke the trust or change the trustee at any time.

Upon the death of the grantor, the trust becomes irrevocable, meaning that the terms of the trust cannot thereafter be changed. The trust property is held, administered, and distributed as if it had passed under the grantor's will through probate and into a testamentary trust. The provisions of the trust agreement which apply to the administration and distribution of the trust assets after the death of the grantor become operative and are carried out immediately. There are no probate delays, and the publicity normally necessary to the probate of a will is dispensed with.

A revocable living trust has a number of advantages and only a few minor disadvantages when compared with a testamentary trust.

### Advantages of the Revocable Trust

#### Management Uninterrupted by Incapacity

If a bank or an experienced person is selected as trustee of a revocable living trust, and a large part or all of the grantor's assets are placed in the trust during his lifetime, the revocable trust can afford continuous experienced management of the trust assets regardless of the grantor's physical or mental incapacity. If the grantor of the trust desires to retain investment control of the trust assets, the trust agreement can provide that while the grantor is alive and remains competent, no purchases or sales of the trust assets or any other important actions can be made without his approval. Should the grantor become unable to manage his assets, either through mental or physical disabilities, the revocable trust is the ideal instrument for continuing proper management.

In contrast, a power of attorney given to another person to manage the grantor's affairs will be automatically revoked upon the grantor's mental incapacity if the power of attorney does not contain the words "This power of attorney shall not terminate on disability of the principal" or similar words, and will be automatically revoked upon the appointment and qualification of a guardian. Proceedings for the appointment of a guardian for the property of a person upon his becoming senile or incompetent, or upon his drifting in and out of lucid mental periods can provoke unpleasant family quarrels. It certainly will involve court control of the assets of the incompetent, large legal and bonding fees, severe restrictions on investments, and much red tape.

The revocable living trust is the answer to these problems. The trustee can perform all of the necessary management of the trust assets, including the collection of income, the purchase and sale of trust assets, and the management of a closely held business or real estate. In addition the trustee can make payment of hospital, nursing and doctor bills, and other expenses of the grantor. When the period of temporary crisis ends, the trust can be revoked by the grantor if he so desires, or the grantor may again take up active management of his trust assets while leaving the assets with the trustee. If the grantor dies, the trust can act as the grantor's will insofar as the assets of the trust are concerned.

## Management for the Busy Executive or Professional

A revocable trust is a valuable aid to the busy executive or professional person who does not have time to study the stock market or to do the many other things that are involved in managing the investment of valuable trust assets. A bank can supply experienced investment guidance and free a busy executive or professional person from worries that might interfere with the pursuit of his business or profession, while at the same time assuring him of continuous expert investment management of his trust assets.

## Segregation of Assets

A revocable trust also has the advantage of preventing certain properties from becoming mingled with other property. For example, if a wife has inherited property from her parents, and she desires that the property be kept separate from community property of her husband, she can place her separate property with a bank in a revocable trust. The trustee can maintain adequate records to keep that property segregated from the community assets.

## Trial Run for the Trustee

The revocable living trust allows the grantor to observe the operation of the bank or person that he desires to manage his estate upon his death. The grantor can then satisfy himself as to the manner in which his assets will be managed and administered after his death. This will also allow his wife to become familiar with his trust officer and lawyer, so that old friends, instead of strangers, will be there to take care of his wife at his death.

### Privacy of Disposition of Assets at Death

Another advantage of the revocable trust is the privacy afforded the grantor for the disposition of his estate at his death. Assets placed in a revocable living trust do not become a matter of public court record as is the case with a probated will. Newspaper publicity about the grantor's assets, his beneficiaries, and his disposition plans are thus avoided.

### Reduction of Probate Expense

A revocable living trust may result in the reduction of probate expenses. Executor's commissions, attorney's fees, accounting fees, appraiser's fees, and other charges arising from the administration of a deceased person's estate are based to a certain extent on the value of the assets passing under the decedent's will. Keeping property out of the probate or testamentary estate of the grantor can reduce such charges. If all of a grantor's assets are in a revocable trust at the time of his death, it may not be necessary to go through probate at all. However, this reduction may be offset to some degree by the cost of the trustee's administering the trust assets during the grantor's lifetime. The desire to save probate expense should not normally be the controlling reason for creating a revocable living trust.

### Avoidance of Will Contest

A revocable trust is less vulnerable to attack by disgruntled heirs than is a will. It is rather easy for a relative to attack the probate of a will, even when the attack is based on flimsy reasons. It is quite expensive and time consuming for the executor to win a total victory in such a contest.

An attack can be made on a revocable living trust on the same grounds used to contest a will (lack of capacity or undue influence).

However, such a contest does not tie up the trust assets in the same manner as a will contest ties up the probate assets. The burden of proof seems to lie more heavily with the trust contester, as the attacks are more often successful with wills than with living trusts. The reason for this is that a will is merely a piece of paper until the testator's death. Nothing in a will has any effect or substance until after the will has been admitted to probate by a formal court order, and all assets are tied up until the will contest is settled. By contrast a trust is in full force and effect at the moment of death of the grantor, and if there is a contest of the trust, the trustee has assets in his hands with which to pay for a defense of the trust.

## Uninterrupted Management at Death

A revocable living trust provides a means for avoiding any interruption in the management of the trust's assets upon the death of the grantor. Stocks, securities, real estate, and so on can continue to be managed, and debts, expenses of last illness, funeral bills, taxes, and so on can be paid without interruption. Further, there is no delay incurred in providing for the grantor's family immediately after his death. This elimination of delay is important when the trust property consists of assets which require day-to-day handling to avoid loss, and when the family has immediate financial requirements upon the death of the grantor.

## Avoidance of Probate in Other States

If the grantor owns property physically located in different states, it may be possible to avoid expensive and time-consuming probate proceedings in these states by conveying the property to a trustee during the grantor's lifetime. However, if real estate in other states is to be placed in a revocable living trust, it is important to make sure that the laws of the state where the property is located allow a trustee from another state to act within that state.

## Tax Treatment of the Revocable Trust

Assets in a revocable living trust are taxable under the federal income tax, estate, and gift tax laws, and the Texas inheritance tax laws in the same manner as property owned outright by the grantor. No gift tax is payable when a grantor creates a revocable living trust. During his lifetime all of the income of the trust is taxed to him, and upon his death, all of the property in the trust is included in his estate for federal estate and Texas inheritance tax purposes. After his death the trust becomes irrevocable, and the same tax advantages available to testamentary trusts are available to living trusts. These include the use of the unlimited marital deduction trust and the avoidance of federal estate and Texas inheritance tax on up to $600,000 of assets by using the credit shelter trust.

## Disadvantages of the Revocable Trust

### Loss of Probate Estate as Tax Entity

To the extent that assets have been placed in a living trust, the use of the probate estate as a separate tax entity having its own tax bracket is unavailable. Often, through good planning, payment of income tax of an estate can be delayed by strategic timing on distributions from the probate estate to a trust and eventually to a beneficiary. Of course, without the probate estate, this advantage is somewhat diminished.

### Limitation on Amount of Discounted Treasury Bonds Accepted at Par for Estate Tax Payment

Certain U.S. Treasury bonds which were purchased at a discount can be redeemed at par plus accrued interest at the death of the owner, for the purpose of having the proceeds applied on the payment of federal estate taxes. Such bonds held by a revocable living trust are redeemable only in the amount up to the amount of the federal estate tax which the trustee of the trust is required to pay under the terms of the trust instrument. Therefore, it may be desirable to keep the ownership of such bonds in the name of the owner himself, rather than to place them in a revocable trust.

*Application of the "Unlimited Throwback Rule"*

The option to accumulate income in the estate during the period of administration without incurring the unlimited throwback rule is an income tax provision available to an estate but not to a trust. The rule taxes some of the income to the beneficiaries of a trust upon later distribution of assets to the beneficiaries.

*Community Property and Revocable Trusts*

If community property is to be placed in a revocable trust, the wife should join the husband in the execution of the trust agreement, or the trust may not be allowed to continue after the death of the husband. This ruling was established under the March 13, 1968, decision of the Texas Supreme Court in the case of *Land vs. Marshall.*

### Summary

By using a revocable living trust, a person may select a trustee to manage his assets in the event he should become incapacitated, rather than having a person appointed by the court to do so. While competent, the grantor can continue to manage his assets, even though they are placed in a revocable living trust, or he may turn complete management over to the trustee. The creation of the trust during the grantor's lifetime allows him to study the management of his assets by the trustee to be sure that the trustee will handle them in the proper manner after his death. The management of the property placed in a revocable living trust is uninterrupted at death. Such continuity may be particularly important when the property managed is a closely held business needing constant attention. By placing property owned in other states in a revocable living trust, probate within those states may be avoided.

# 16

# Will Substitutes—
# Life Insurance

*Exemption from Creditors*

Life insurance is something no one really wants but which the head of almost every family has. It is usually a large part of the average man's estate. As a result, laws have been passed to favor and encourage the purchase of life insurance policies. One of the most favorable benefits given to policy holders is that the proceeds of life insurance are exempt from creditors' claims. In Texas, unless the proceeds are payable to the estate or the executor of the insured, the death benefits of a life insurance policy are exempt from the claims of the decedent's creditors or even the beneficiary's creditors. In addition, the cash surrender value of a life insurance policy which has been in force for more than two years is exempt from creditors' claims during the insured's life to the extent that the beneficiaries are members of the insured's family or are dependents of an insured single person.

Thus, if a person dies leaving debts or a lawsuit against his estate resulting in a judgment against him, his life insurance will be available to support his surviving spouse and orphaned children (assuming the decedent named them as beneficiaries). The only exception to this is a claim for unpaid income, gift, or estate taxes due the federal government. The "sovereign" never loses.

### Types of Life Insurance Policies

While there are many types of life insurance policies, the two most common are ordinary life and term policies.

The *ordinary life policy* is a permanent contract with an even (non-increasing) cost to the purchaser based on his age at the time he takes out the policy. But when the owner reaches an age (e.g., age 60), when his children have grown up and left home, his house has been paid for, and in general his obligations are less than they were at, say, age 35, he may choose to stop paying on the ordinary life policies and still be well off. He can elect to take paid-up insurance on a smaller amount of death proceeds, or he can cash in some of his policies.

The *term policy* is paid for at one rate during each term (1–5 years) for which it is purchased. It is cheaper than ordinary life insurance, but as each term expires it costs more to renew since the owner will be older and more likely to die during the particular term for which the company has agreed to take the risk.

### Methods of Paying Proceeds

If the insured knows to whom he wants the death benefits to be paid, he must decide how he wants them paid.

The life policy will generally provide four principal settlement options at death. These are the interest option, the fixed-period option, the fixed-amount option, and the life-annuity option.

Under the *interest option*, the beneficiary leaves the death proceeds with the insurance company. The company pays interest at a minimum guaranteed rate on the amount of the proceeds on some periodical date, such as monthly, quarterly, twice a year, or annually. Companies usually pay interest at a higher rate than the contract calls for. The beneficiary can draw out some or all of the proceeds in addition to the interest at any reasonable time until all of the proceeds are gone.

The *fixed-period option* pays out a portion of the proceeds plus interest earned on the balance held by the company. This could be in 10 annual installments or 240 monthly installments or any other number of payments over a fixed period of time. If the company is told how long the beneficiary wants the proceeds to last, it can advise the number of payments the beneficiary can take out over that time and how much each payment will be.

The *fixed-amount option* is quite similar to the fixed-period option. The beneficiary tells the company how much he would like to receive each month out of the proceeds and interest which the proceeds will be earning while the company is holding the proceeds. The company will advise how many payments in the amount the beneficiary has requested can be made until the policy proceeds are exhausted. While the fixed-period and fixed-amount options are similar, the fixed-amount option is more flexible for the beneficiary and the company. The amount of the payment will remain the same under the fixed-amount option even if the total proceeds available become greater due to increased interest payments made voluntarily by the company or because the total proceeds have become smaller because of a principal withdrawal. It is the number of such installments which will increase or decrease. There are many other policy advantages of the fixed-amount option over the fixed-period option.

Finally, there is the *life-annuity option*. Here the company keeps the proceeds and pays at least the rate of interest guaranteed and usually the higher current rate it can pay at its option. The company pays this total amount out in installments based on the life expectancy of the beneficiary or on the life expectancies of two beneficiaries. Almost all companies today will guarantee to pay the beneficiary of the policy an installment each month for the rest of the beneficiary's life and in no case less than 120 monthly payments or 240 monthly payments. This guards against forfeiture of the rest of the proceeds because of early death of the beneficiary.

## Income Tax Benefit

Congress has provided a very useful tax benefit for owners of life insurance. The death benefits are exempted from the income tax. It makes no difference how the beneficiary receives the proceeds (i.e., lump sum, 240 monthly installments, or a life annuity) or how many premiums were paid by the insured. No income tax is due on the considerable economic gain which has resulted. The actual premiums paid for a $10,000, 10-year paid-up policy will be much less than the $10,000 death benefit. There will be a very large interest factor being built up and compounded over the life of the insured to allow the insurance company to pay off the proceeds later. This is almost like putting money in a savings account and compounding the interest over the years. With a savings account, income tax is paid each year on the interest earned. Not so with a life insurance policy. Although largely unheralded today and perhaps unappreciated in advance of the receipt of death proceeds, it is a true advantage of insurance over other assets.

A second tax benefit from life insurance comes only to widows or widowers whose spouse died before October 23, 1986. If such a surviving spouse has taken one of the installment options (i.e., fixed period, fixed amount, or annuity), the company may still be paying interest on the proceeds which it holds. All or part of this interest will come to such a beneficiary tax-free as installments or principal are received. The installments are partly current interest and partly matured proceeds. Congress allows such a beneficiary to receive up to $1,000 in interest each year tax-free when earned on proceeds left with the company. This tax benefit does not apply if the beneficiary has taken the interest option. In 1986, the Congress, searching for more money to pay for its expanded spending, classified this "widow's mite" as a "tax dodge" and eliminated it for widows of insureds who died after October 22, 1986.

## How Should a Beneficiary Take Proceeds?

This decision is one of the most important a beneficiary must make, and yet there is no absolute answer. Most people should consider taking enough of the proceeds through an installment option to provide at least $1,000 per year in tax-exempt income. There is an easy formula which insurance companies will furnish for computing the amount which must be left with the insurance company under an installment option to take full advantage of this $1,000 annual income tax exemption.

After deciding to take this tax advantage, the beneficiary still faces the question of whether to take all the other proceeds in a lump sum or an annuity. While most insurance companies are currently guaranteeing 4% interest on their payments (although they are actually paying 8–9%) and while most people can get at least 5¼% from a savings account, greater risk is involved in the purchase of corporate stock or other security investments. If one has only a modest amount of proceeds available and cannot be certain that it will be enough no matter how long he lives, he should probably select an annuity option for the insurance proceeds, although he might be able to make more money in other investments.

### Who Should Decide How Proceeds Are to Be Paid?

Either the decedent during his life or the beneficiary after the decedent's death can decide how the policy proceeds will be disbursed. Which decision should be made depends on the financial situation of the decedent at death and on the ability of the beneficiary either to make the best decision after the decedent's death or to obtain the best advice available.

It is difficult for one person to decide at age 30 what will be best for his beneficiary at age 70. It is therefore often better to let the beneficiary decide after the decedent's death because the beneficiary can make a decision based on the situation at that time. Yet, there are reasons for having the decedent select the option. If the beneficiary is incapacitated, has no business judgment, or is a spendthrift, the decedent may wish to select the option during his lifetime. If the decedent makes this determination, he should review the situation with his life underwriter every few years.

### Life Insurance Trust

The decedent can name a bank or an independent trust company as trustee of his insurance proceeds and give the corporate trustee wide discretion in assisting the beneficiary after his death. To accomplish this, a trust is created and the corporate trustee is named beneficiary of the insurance. Life insurance transferred to a life insurance trust is included in the estate of the insured if death occurs within three years. To avoid this, the trust should be the applicant owner and beneficiary of the life insurance policy.

In most cases, the corporate trustee's trust department will be a wise choice as the beneficiary holding the insurance proceeds. The beneficiary may act as the trustee and so may related and unrelated persons. Who is really qualified to take the place of the deceased? The corporate trustee is qualified through experience, education, and facilities to handle personal business problems which can arise after the death. With the flexibility of the insurance policy, the insurance company can meet some of the business and human problems, but the insurance company cannot use its discretion to change the amount of money to be spent for each child's unique health, education, or maintenance problems. Many factors weigh in favor of an insurance trust, although they are not for everyone.

## Gifts of Policies

A complete gift of a policy can be made. A decedent may make an absolute gift of every right, power, and privilege and of all incidents of ownership in a policy to the beneficiary or to a trustee of a trust for the benefit of the beneficiary and then his children, or to his church or college. If he makes an absolute and irrevocable gift of a policy at least three years prior to his death, then the proceeds will not be included in his taxable estate for federal estate tax purposes. Many reasons exist for giving a policy away during one's lifetime.

For a decedent with enough property to be concerned with the estate tax, the best reason for giving away his insurance policies to his family is to eliminate the estate tax which his estate will pay on his portion of the life insurance. However, when he gives away the life insurance, he loses the use of the cash values and the rights to borrow on the policies. His estate also loses the cash funds it would receive at his death. Of course, if he names his spouse or his adult children as policy beneficiaries or gives them the policies as absolute gifts, they can lend his estate money or buy assets from his estate at their date-of-death values. This procedure could provide the estate with cash to pay estate costs and the federal estate and Texas inheritance taxes. The same thing can be accomplished by giving the trustee of a life insurance trust the power and authority, but not the duty, to lend the estate money or to buy assets from the estate.

Gifts of policies are subject to the federal gift tax. The value of a life insurance policy for gift tax purposes is the cost of replacing it. This is an amount quite close to the cash value of the policy, although the technical term is the "policy terminal reserve." If there is no cash value, the value of the gift is usually small and is not related to the size of the death benefit.

## Tax-Saving Life Insurance Gifts

The basic insurance gift plan is to have the decedent merely assign all of his interest in a life insurance policy outright to a beneficiary.

This puts the policy proceeds out of his estate at his death. This can be done by using forms (which should be reviewed for their legal effect in Texas) furnished by the insurance companies.

In most cases where estate taxes will cause family concern and the family has only modest means other than life insurance, the decedent can create a life insurance trust to which he makes absolute gifts of the insurance policies on his life. He may name a spouse as the trust's income beneficiary for life with the proceeds continuing in trust for his children after the spouse's death, or with the proceeds going outright to his grown children after the spouse's death. He can give the trustee the power and the right to lend funds to his estate or to buy assets from his estate. During his lifetime decedent can continue to pay the premiums on these gift policies after he makes the gift with only slight gift tax on the death benefits. At the spouse's later death, however, half of the trust will probably be included in her estate.

## A Word of Caution

Life insurance is not part of the probate estate, unless the estate or executor is named as beneficiary of the policy or unless a beneficiary is not named. Just because it is possible to avoid passing some or all of one's property, including life insurance, to beneficiaries without it passing through probate does not mean that it should be done. Texas probate costs are moderate, and many hoped-for savings in avoiding probate are much more apparent than real. Costs can be avoided when probate is eliminated, but other costs can be incurred in creating trusts and other tax-avoidance devices.

## Summary

Life insurance involves using current funds to provide for later needs. The principal factor working against building an estate is lack of time. Life insurance provides the time needed and the tax-free accumulation of interest to create the capital. If one lives long enough, saves enough, and does not pay income taxes on interest being earned, he will accumulate the means to provide for his later years and the welfare of his family. If he dies early, insurance takes the place of the time he lost, and the financial welfare of his family is assured.

# 17

# Probate and Tax Savings Through Gifts

Gift giving often plays a part in passing property from one generation to the next, even without the motivation of estate planning. Parents may transfer an interest in the family business to their children in order to increase the children's interest in the enterprise and to equip them to assume the responsibilities of management. Farmers and ranchers often give their children a few head of livestock so that they may acquire experience in animal husbandry or have an opportunity to build a herd of their own over the years. Husbands often place securities in trust to assure income for their wives. Parents may do the same for the protection of their children.

In addition, gifts often have the benefit of reducing income and estates taxes, as well as lowering the costs of probate. In planning gifts, however, the welfare of the person making the gift and of the welfare of the one receiving it should be the paramount considerations. An older person should not make gifts that would impair his security, his capacity to provide for himself, or his opportunity to continue useful and gainful employment. A child should not be given funds or property which he is too young to handle. The selection and timing of gifts to young people who lack experience in financial management should be designed to further their proper training and development, with adequate provisions for the care and management of property. A desire to effect a tax savings or to avoid probate costs should be secondary considerations when compared with the value of the property involved. It is better to provide for the payment of taxes and other costs by additional life insurance or some other method than to make gifts which would prejudice the security of the giver or be unsuited to the position of the receiver.

There are a number of different ways that gifts may be made. If gifts are made to a minor or to an incompetent, a guardian may be appointed by the county judge to administer the estate of the recipient. Statutes have been enacted under which certain gifts may be made to a "custodian" who holds the property for a minor. In addition, there are various types of trusts which are commonly used.

## Guardianship To Be Avoided

Gifts which come under the administration of guardians often result in legal problems and therefore may not be desirable. Guardianship laws are designed to provide the maximum protection for the child. Annual court accountings are required. In addition, unless the guardian is a bank or trust company, the guardian must post a bond and is severely restricted in investing his ward's funds. These and other provisions may occasion expense and complications. Thus, the management of property by guardians tends to be inflexible, cumbersome, and expensive as well.

## Custodial Arrangements

Custodial arrangements were devised as a simplified means of allowing an adult to hold and manage property for a minor. The custodian does not have to post a bond and the procedure for establishing a custodial arrangement is very simple. A person desiring to make a gift under the custodianship provisions simply makes the gift to Arnold Adult as custodian for Charles Child. In recent years the powers of a custodian have been enlarged to allow investments in securities, real property, tangible personal property, life insurance, and, of course, money. The custodianship, however, is still less flexible than a trust arrangement because it is automatically dissolved when the child reaches the age of majority, whereas a trust can terminate at any age stipulated in the trust instrument. Also, under a custodianship, if the child dies before reaching the age of majority all of the property must go to his estate. This is not required in a trust agreement, for the trust instrument may stipulate exactly to whom the property is to go if the child dies before the trust is terminated.

During the term of the custodianship, the custodian has complete freedom to sell the property and reinvest the proceeds in permissible investments. He has complete discretion on how the property will be used subject to the limitation that it must be used for the benefit of the minor.

When a person names *himself* custodian for another, as in the case of a father for his child, the gift will be included in the taxable estate of the giver, so it is usually best to name someone other than the person making the gift as the custodian.

### Gifts in Trust

For hundreds of years the gift in trust has been the accepted method of making gifts where an outright gift is inappropriate. In almost every case this method is preferable to a gift to a guardian and is generally more flexible than a custodianship. In a trust the giver can specify the rules he desires applied to the management of the property given and to the use of the property by the beneficiary. The terms of the trust may be more or less stringent than a custodianship or guardianship, and provisions may be inserted for many eventualities. The preparation of a trust requires the services of a lawyer, but the cost of these services ordinarily will be a small fraction of the value of the property involved and the income it produces. An individual may serve as a trustee. If a bank or trust company serves as the trustee, the fees normally will be no higher than in the case of comparable services from a guardian or custodian. The legal expenses involved in the establishment and operation of a trust should be materially less than those involved in a guardianship covering the same amount of property. In any individual case, however, the alternative advantages and disadvantages of various modes of making gifts will involve legal issues on which competent advice can be obtained only from a professional who is familiar with trust matters.

### Gifts Save Taxes

Prior to 1977, substantial tax savings could be gained by passing property from one generation to the next by making lifetime gifts rather than by simply letting the property pass through the estate at the time of death. If a person made gifts to his descendants, the property would usually be out of his taxable estate. The gift tax on such gifts was generally significantly lower than the estate tax which would have resulted had no gift been made. The Tax Reform Act of 1976, however, eliminated the bonus of lower gift tax brackets as a tax incentive for major gift giving. Now, for purposes of determining the size of a person's estate, most gifts will be treated as if they had never been made, while any gift tax paid on the gift will be credited against the estate tax due. Nevertheless, although the major tax advantage of gift giving, the lower tax brackets, has been eliminated, there are still some significant tax advantages to be obtained by lifetime gifts.

One tax advantage to lifetime gifts is that, although generally the value of a gift made during the donor's life will be included in determining the size of his total taxable estate upon his death, if the item has appreciated in value between the time the gift was made and the time the donor died, then that appreciation will not be included in the estate. For example, if a parent were to give to his children land worth $100,000 at the time the gift was made, but over the years the land appreciated in value so that when the parent died the land was worth $150,000, then only $100,000 would be reincluded in his taxable estate and the $50,000 of appreciated value would escape taxation. If the gift had not been made then the entire $150,000 worth of land would have been included in the parents' taxable estate. Thus, giving away assets likely to appreciate in value over the years still has tax advantages. The other side of the coin, however, is that the taxpayer should avoid giving away property likely to decrease in value over the years, because the value of the property at the date of gift will be included in the donor's estate no matter what the value of the property at the date of his death. If the property in the preceding example had decreased in value to $50,000, then the $100,000 value would still be included in the taxable estate, whereas if the gift had not been made, then only $50,000 worth of property would have been included in the taxable estate. This will make for an extremely unhappy taxpayer.

A second tax advantage of lifetime gifts is that the money used to pay gift tax is not included in the donor's estate when he dies. Going back to our preceding example, if the parent had paid a $30,000 gift tax on the gift of $100,000 worth of land, then that $30,000 would not be left to be taxed when he died. However, under the new law where that $100,000 gift must be reincluded in the taxable estate, the $30,000 of gift tax paid will be credited against the estate tax due and, therefore, the taxpayer is using tax free dollars to pay his estate tax. If no gift had been made, then the $30,000 which would have been used to pay a gift tax would be left in his taxable estate and subject to estate tax.

If the donor dies within three years of the date of the gift, special rules affect the advantages discussed previously. Prior to 1982, the rule was that any gift made within three years of death was included in the donor's estate and, in addition, the gift tax paid on the subject gift was reincluded in the estate. This means that the gift, including appreciation and the amount used to pay the gift tax, would not escape estate taxation if death occurred within three years of the gift.

After 1981, with certain exceptions, the three-year rule will not apply to those estates, and post-gift appreciation will not be subject to transfer tax. The major exception to this rule concerns gifts of life insurance policies within three years of the donor's death. It is still the rule that gift taxes paid on gifts within three years of death are included in the donor's estate.

A third way that gift giving can save estate taxes is with the annual exclusion. Each person may now make gifts of up to $10,000 a year to any number of people tax free. Moreover, such annual exclusion gifts will not be reincluded in the donor's estate as other gifts are. Thus, all such gifts will escape both gift and estate taxation. The provision for an annual exclusion was originally included to permit normal periodic gifts such as wedding and Christmas presents among family members and friends without the discouraging effect of taxes. The exclusion is $10,000 *per donee,* so the amount that can be given away, tax free, under this provision is limited only by the number of persons to whom gifts are made. For example a man with four children could make gifts to the next generation of up to $40,000 a year tax free. If he were joined by his wife who agreed to combine her exclusion with his, then together they could give away $80,000 a year to their children tax free. As you can see, if a husband and wife were to establish such a gift giving program, then over a period of 10 years they could divest themselves, tax free, of the quite substantial sum of $800,000 worth of property. The power of a husband and wife to combine their exclusions applies even though the property given might be the separate property of either spouse. Such annual exclusion-giving programs can be very attractive.

To qualify for the annual exclusion, gifts must be made in a manner which gives the recipient immediate access to the gift. Thus, with a few exceptions, most gifts intended to qualify for the annual exclusion must be made outright or to custodians and cannot be made in trust. An important exception to this rule is that the annual exclusion may be used when a gift is made in trust for a child, if the trust terminates when the child reaches age 21 and if the trust contains certain other provisions required by the Internal Revenue Code. These provisions include a requirement that distributions of income and principal be made only to or for the benefit of the child. Such trusts may be included in the estate of the donor for estate tax purposes if the donor serves as trustee, unless carefully drafted from a legal standpoint. Such an arrangement works well when a grandparent desires to make a gift in trust to a grandchild and appoints his child as the trustee. A second exception is that the annual exclusion may also be used when gifts are made to a trust that can be revoked by the beneficiary or when the beneficiary or beneficiary's legal guardian has the right to demand a distribution in the amount of the gift. Such demand rights are generally limited in time to 30 or 60 days after receipt of notice of a gift from the trustee. For tax purposes such gifts are considered equivalent to outright gifts to the beneficiary. A competent legal advisor can devise a trust that may extend well past the age of 21 as a practical matter, although legally the beneficiary may have the right to terminate the trust at age 21 or to demand a distribution for a limited period following a gift.

A fourth factor to keep in mind in evaluating the tax advantages of gifts is the unified system of tax credits. The tax law provides up to $192,800 in tax credits that can be applied against the gift tax during a person's lifetime. Because a gift of around $600,000 will incur a tax of about $192,800, a taxpayer is able to give away as much as $600,000 during his life without paying a tax at the time the gifts are made.

Of course, the tax will come at the time of death when the gifts are reincluded in the taxable estate. This still provides a significant benefit, if a person desires to give away property that is worth less than $600,000 at the time of the gift but is expected to rapidly appreciate. Remembering the case of the parent who gave away land worth $100,000 at the time of the gift but worth $150,000 at the time of his death, you can see that he could obtain the benefit of removing $50,000 worth of appreciation from his taxable estate without any transfer tax cost.

One last tax advantage of lifetime gifts that must be considered is the income and estate tax savings that may result from transferring income producing property from a high-bracket taxpayer to a low-bracket tax-payer. Before the income tax rate reductions enacted in 1986, these savings could be substantial. For example, under pre-1987 law, if a parent were a 50-percent-bracket income taxpayer and his child were a 20-per-cent-bracket income taxpayer, then a gift of property that produced a $5,000-a-year income would result in a $15,000 income tax savings to the family over a period of 10 years. If the parent had kept the gift he would have had $50,000 of income and paid $25,000 in income tax but after the gift, the child will pay only $10,000 in income tax on the same $50,000 income. The 1986 Tax Reform Act reduced tax rates so that beginning in 1988 the maximum rate is 28%. It also provides that gift income distributed to a child under age 14 is taxed at the parent's rate. In the past, often the income tax savings alone prompted such gifts. Under the new income tax rates, the savings are no longer as significant since there are only two rates—15% and 28%—a difference of only 13%. However, some savings may still be made and there is always the unfortunate prospect of higher rates in the future.

Prior to 1986, a common device to accomplish this shifting of income but yet retaining the right to get the principal back after a period of time was a short-term trust commonly known as the Clifford Trust. Generally, it required the principal to be left in trust for at least 10 years before it can terminate. This device was quite successful in financing children's college educations or providing for the support of elderly parents who need help, because it shifted income to the lower tax brackets of the people who are going to get the money anyway, yet the principal is not given away permanently. Effective for trusts created on or after March 1, 1986, if the person creating the trust retains a right to get the trust property back at the end of the trust term, and the value of that interest is more than 5% of the trust value, all the income is taxed to the grantor. Under the I.R.S. tables, it would have to stay in trust for over 30 years to have a value under 5%. This in effect eliminates the use of this short term Clifford Trust technique for shifting income.

As an added bonus, even under the new laws, any income produced from gift property will not be included in the donor's taxable estate. If the parent with property producing income of $5,000 a year transferred it to a trust for a child 10 years before the parent's death, then $50,000 (less income taxes), which would have been in the parent's taxable estate had he kept the property, would not be in the parent's taxable estate.

### How Gift Tax is Figured

When gifts exceed the annual exclusion, a gift tax return must be filed. The gift tax is computed on a cumulative basis. When taxable gifts are made, the amount of the tax is determined by calculating the gift tax due on an amount equal to all past and current gifts and subtracting from it the tax that would be due on all past gifts. For this reason, gift tax brackets increase as taxable gifts are made. For example, if a single person with no prior gifts makes a gift of $50,000 to one person, then he has made a gift subject to taxation in the amount of $40,000 ($50,000 less the $10,000 annual exclusion). The gift tax on such an amount is $8,200. If he made a similar gift of $50,000 the next year, his gift tax would be calculated as follows:

| | |
|---|---|
| Total taxable gifts made to that date | $80,000 |
| Gift tax on $80,000 taxable gift | $18,200 |
| Less gift tax on $40,000 taxable gift | 8,200 |
| Gift tax on the gift in the second year | $10,000 |

Note that the first year's gift was taxed at a top bracket of 22 percent but the second year's gift was taxed at a top bracket of 26 percent. Of course, no tax would actually have been paid in either year because the taxpayer would use $8,200 of his tax credits the first year and $10,000 the next year. Remember, however, that the tax is merely deferred, because a gift in excess of the annual exclusion will be reincluded in the donor's estate tax computation when he dies. The tax on the same amount of gifts made by a married couple instead of a single person will be roughly half, because of the married couple's ability to split their gifts. The gift tax bracket has under current cases a maximum rate of 55 percent reducing to 50 percent in 1988.

### Primary Considerations in Making a Gift

Because the best interests of the family members or other beneficiaries of the trust should be the paramount consideration, it is often best to incorporate into a trust those provisions that provide the best family scheme, even if it requires the payment of some tax. Each individual should weigh with his counselor the tax benefit against the amount of control the donor must give up to obtain that tax benefit.

In any event, if property or appreciation in property given in trust is to be removed from the estate of the donor for estate tax purposes, the gift must be irrevocable, and the donor must part with the right to receive income from it. Furthermore, the donor must forego the right to determine how trust benefits will be shared among the beneficiaries. This may be accomplished in a trust of which the donor is trustee. However, it is usually desirable to utilize an independent trustee where gifts in trust are made by a living person and estate tax considerations are important. The variations in arrangements that will meet the various tax requirements are numerous, and the controlling rules are technical and complex. Therefore, the lawyer who drafts such instruments must develop a recommendation in each case that will comply with such rules while fulfilling family needs.

The estate plan must also consider the generation-skipping tax, which was greatly expanded by the 1986 Tax Reform Act. This new law imposes an additional transfer tax in addition to the gift tax on gifts to grandchildren whether direct or in trust with the children receiving a life income interest. Exceptions apply for gifts qualifying for the annual exclusion ($10,000 or less) and each donor has a $1,000,000 lifetime exception. There is also a special exemption of $2,000,000 per grandchild for qualifying gifts made before 1990. Any time gifts are made to grandchildren, either outright or interest, these complex rules on the generation-skipping tax need to be considered.

A variety of specialized techniques may be considered in larger estates where estate tax problems are especially critical. It may be helpful to combine a gift with a sale of property to one's children by selling property that has appreciated in value at its original cost. The seller will ordinarily realize no taxable gain from such a sale, and the amount of the gift will be the difference between the property value and the sales price. Property may be sold to children or others for its actual value with the purchase price payable in installments. The payment of the installments may be forgiven or cancelled as they become due. This approach is more practical where there has been no substantial appreciation in the property's value from the time it was acquired by the seller because there can be adverse income tax consequences.

Special types of gifts may be desirable to permit a spouse or child to carry insurance on the life of the working spouse. Such gifts may enable the family to keep the insurance proceeds out of the taxable estate at the breadwinner's death and yet have liquid funds available for payment of taxes or for other needs. Trusts for the purpose of owning such insurance are subject to special provisions of the tax laws and must be separately considered.

A technique for making gifts that is growing in popularity is the Grantor Retained Income Trust or GRIT. In a GRIT, the Grantor of the trust retains the right to the income for a fixed period of time. Because the Grantor is keeping the income, the value of the gift to the remainder beneficiary is discounted by the value of the retained income interest. This discounting can result in significant transfer tax savings. For example, in a ten year trust using a 10% discount factor (the discount rate is adopted by the IRS each month based on government interest rates), the value of the gift will be about 38.5% of the trust property. To avoid estate tax problems, the Grantor's interest in the trust needs to be a "qualified trust income interest" as defined by the estate tax law. This law stipulates that the trust cannot last over ten years; only the donor can have an income interest in the property in the trust; and that the donor cannot be a trustee. If the donor should die during the period of the GRIT, the value of the GRIT property will be included in the donor's estate and most of the tax benefits will be lost. However, for donors who are in good health and can expect to outlive the term of the GRIT, use of such a trust can produce substantial transfer tax savings. In many cases, term insurance can also be purchased for the term of the GRIT to protect against the contingency of the death of the grantor during the term of the trust.

Where larger amounts of property are involved, other types of special arrangements may be required. It may be desirable to change the form of organization of the parents' business to create interests that are easily transferred by gift. For example, voting rights and other factors affecting stock in a family enterprise may be modified so that shares are created that are appropriate for gift purposes. In such circumstances special consideration must be given to the effect that such stock provisions may have on the valuation of the shares. In other cases a family limited partnership might be desirable. The parents could be the general partners and the children the limited partners, allowing centralized management of family properties but relative ease in transferring ownership interests. Each situation presents different problems and there is no ready-made solution for all. In addition, there are new tax rules designed to prevent "estate freezes." For these reasons the development of an appropriate solution in an individual case should take into consideration the economic and tax positions of the parties, the proper management of the property, and above all the best interests of the persons involved.

# 18

# The Irrevocable Trust

The *irrevocable trust* is one that the creator of the trust cannot revoke or alter. The creator of a trust during lifetime is called a "settlor," while a creator under a will is called a "testator." For convenience, this chapter will always refer to the creator as a settlor. The settlor of the trust has given up the right to change his/her mind and has relinquished the trust property either permanently or for some specific period of time. An irrevocable trust may be created by will or during the lifetime of the settlor. It may result from a revocable trust, which by its terms becomes irrevocable upon the death of the settlor.

### Why Trusts?

Since the irrevocable trust by definition involves a more permanent form of arrangement than the revocable trust, it seems wise to consider at least briefly some basic background information concerning trusts. A trust is simply a device in which the legal title to property and the right to control it are separated from the right to receive the benefits from it. Historically, the need for such a separation arose from the plight of the man with property who wanted to make provision for his family or friends but feared giving property directly to them because of their inexperience in financial management or their irresponsibility. He solved this problem by placing the legal title and management of the property in the hands of a third party whom he considered responsible. He then stipulated the manner in which the benefits were to be paid to his beneficiary.

The assurance of proper financial management is probably the most important reason for the existence of trusts. Who should be selected as trustee to exercise this management? This decision is much more important in an irrevocable trust than in a revocable trust. Sometimes a person wanting to create a trust has confidence in the judgment and managing abilities of a relative, a friend, or a business associate. But such a person is not always available. Even if he is, he may die or become disabled or his time may be too limited.

The increasing need for reliable and capable trustees has spurred tremendous growth in the size and capability of bank trust departments in Texas in recent years. Almost every bank of substantial size now has a trust department. Although their skill in managing property and investments varies, the close governmental supervision of bank trust department activities assures certain capabilities and inspires confidence in the integrity of banks as trustees. Settlors often find the combination of a bank and an individual as co-trustees is desirable.

In addition to sound financial management, a trust offers its settlor an opportunity for added flexibility in carrying out his desires regarding his beneficiaries. Many variations are available. The classic pattern is for one beneficiary to receive all of the income for life, with the remainder paid at his death to another. The income, as well as the remainder, can be divided among several beneficiaries if that is desirable, and termination can occur at a time other than death. For example, a father might create a trust providing for distribution of the income among his children until the youngest attains age 25. At that time the trust would terminate, and the principal of the trust would be divided among the children. The variations are limitless.

Even with all the possibilities open to the settlor of a trust, he must recognize that the circumstances that inspire his decisions today may change during the term of the trust. The perfect plan of distribution that he creates today may become the straightjacket of tomorrow when unexpected events occur. A trust that irrevocably provides for the equal division of income between two children may seem unfortunate in retrospect if one child accumulates wealth and has great income and the other becomes incapacitated and incapable of supporting himself. The recognition of our inability to see into the future has given rise to better techniques for carrying out the intentions of the settlor.

One method of allowing for the unexpected is to give the trustee discretion in distributing income. The trust instrument may provide that the trustee may either accumulate income in the trust or distribute it to a beneficiary, depending upon the circumstances at the time. The most obvious need for such a provision is in a trust for minors. The amount of money needed for the support of a minor varies greatly as he develops through the years. Usually the decision of how much income to distribute each year can be made best as events unfold. The settlor can specify in the instrument the criteria to be used by the trustee in making distributions (for example, a provision that he wants the trust to provide a standard of living comparable to that enjoyed by the person for whom the trust was created). Or, he may have sufficient confidence in the trustee to follow the often used course of allowing the trustee complete discretion. This same type of discretion can be granted the trustee with respect to making distributions out of the principal of the trust as the need arises. Often the settlor will want the trustee to be able to distribute principal to one or more beneficiaries if circumstances should indicate a need. This can be arranged in the trust instrument. He can set the guidelines for such an occurrence or he can leave it to the judgment of the trustee.

The trustee can also be granted limited or broad power to decide who among a group of beneficiaries will receive distributions of income and principal and how much they will receive. This permits making the decision at the time of the distribution, rather than trying to make it in advance.

Heavy, graduated income and estate taxes have been largely responsible for the enormous increase in the use of trusts even for moderate estates in the past two decades. The wise use of irrevocable trusts can result in substantial savings in estate taxes and, to a lesser extent, in income taxes. Sometimes the saving is only indirectly attributable to the trust device itself. Often a person desiring to effect a saving in that manner is unwilling to make an outright gift to the beneficiary. Only through a trust is he able to satisfy his personal preferences and objectives in a manner that allows him to make the gift and realize the tax benefit. More often the benefit is directly related to the use of the trust device.

Happily for some, the program of trust planning that should be adopted without considering tax benefits is often also the program that produces tax savings. For others, compromises may be necessary in weighing non-tax objectives with tax-saving techniques.

### Tax Advantages of Trusts

Most trusts are created by will, but sometimes it is desirable to anticipate the will by making a gift during the lifetime of the settlor *inter vivos*. Such a gift, if the trust is properly drawn, will remove the property from the settlor's taxable estate (or at least remove the appreciation in value following the date of the gift) and thus effect the same tax savings as outright gifts do. The settlor can reserve no right to receive income or principal from the trust, or the property will be included in his taxable estate in spite of the trust gift. Furthermore, if the settlor retains too much administrative power over the trust, either as a co-trustee or otherwise, he runs the risk of losing the estate tax savings. The safest course from a tax standpoint is for the settlor to rely entirely on an independent trustee and retain no administrative power over the trust for himself.

An estate tax saving more directly related to the trust device is the shielding of the exempt portion of one spouse's estate from imposition of estate taxes upon the surviving spouse's death (see Chapters 5 and 7). While the first spouse to die could eliminate any estate taxes upon his or her death by giving all property to the surviving spouse outright, all of the property would be taxed upon the survivor's death. On the other hand, a bypass trust can hold all or a portion of the property of the first spouse for the benefit of the surviving spouse, but will not be subject to estate taxes upon the survivor's death. The distribution provisions of this "bypass trust" might provide that all income is distributed to the surviving spouse, or might leave distributions to the discretion of the trustee.

Broad flexibility is available with respect to distributions of principal also. The surviving spouse can be given a non-cumulative right to receive each year a distribution of up to $5,000 or 5% of the trust assets, whichever is greater, without jeopardizing the ultimate tax savings. A standard can be set for determining principal distributions, or complete discretion can be left to the trustee. The same plan can be arranged for the settlor's children as well. Finally, if the distribution standards are drafted correctly, the surviving spouse may be named as trustee. In short, the law allows the estate planner plenty of room to tailor the trust to meet the individual needs and desires of a particular settlor without endangering the tax savings. The same rules apply regardless of which spouse dies first. This type of planning can also be effected for any other person the settlor may wish to benefit.

Another type of tax saving from the use of trusts is the income tax savings afforded by *sprinkling trusts* and *multiple trusts*. The sprinkling trust is the trust under which an independent trustee, often a bank, but sometimes a trusted friend or business associate, is given broad discretion to accumulate or distribute income among beneficiaries. A trust of this type is a taxpayer itself, paying tax with its own income tax return on any income not distributed.

Because of the graduated income tax rates, a given amount of income will incur the least amount of tax if it is spread among a maximum number of taxpayers. Suppose, for example, a woman having a husband and three adult sons dies and leaves her half of the community property in three separate trusts—one for each son. The income and principal for each trust can be accumulated or distributed either to the son for whom it is named or to the father. The father has the other half of the community property. If his property proves inadequate for his support, the income from the trusts can be distributed to him. However, if he has adequate funds apart from the trusts in any one or more years, then the income can be retained in the trusts where it may be taxed at a lower bracket. Or some or all of it can be distributed to the sons if they need it. They may be in a low tax bracket. However, if any of the sons is under 14 years of age, income distributed to him will probably be taxed at the father's income tax bracket under the new "kiddie tax." But the important point is that the income can be divided among the father, the three trusts, and the three sons—seven taxpayers—so as to provide maximum tax advantages while taking care of their needs. Income accumulated in a trust and taxed to it can sometimes be subject to more tax when it is distributed, so careful planning is necessary in each case.

The income tax advantages of trusts were reduced in the 1986 overhaul of the tax laws. While the basic scheme of taxation remains intact, the graduated income tax brackets for trusts have been compressed so that trusts reach the maximum income tax bracket after earning only a small amount of income. For example, for the 1988 taxable year, trusts will pay income taxes at the maximum 28% rate for taxable income exceeding $5,000. In addition, the benefits of the 15% tax bracket on the first $5,000 of income is phased out for taxable income between $13,000 and $26,000.

In creating long-term trusts, the settlor should take care in selecting the trustee and in providing for successor trustees. Care should also be taken to give the trustee or trustees broad enough management and investment powers to permit flexible administration of the trust in today's complex economic environment.

## Generation-Skipping Trusts

While most trusts may terminate during the beneficiary's lifetime, at which point the trust assets are distributed outright to the beneficiary, some trusts may last for the beneficiary's lifetime (and beyond). An estate planner can draft the trust so that upon the beneficiary's death, the assets either will be paid outright or continue to be held in trust for the benefit of some other person or persons (usually the beneficiary's descendants), without being subjected to estate taxes in the beneficiary's estate. For example, a father could give property to his children in trust during his lifetime (which would be subject to gift taxes), or could leave the property to his children in trust upon his death (which would be subject to estate taxes). During the children's lifetimes, they could receive distributions from the trust similar to those given the beneficiaries of the bypass trust previously described. Upon the children's deaths, the property held in their trusts would either be paid to their descendants or continue to be held in trust for their descendants. This property would not, however, be subject to estate taxes in the children's estates. If the property had been left outright to the children, then it would have been subject to estate taxes once again upon their deaths. Therefore, the trusts provide a means of skipping estate taxes in an entire generation, and are referred to as "generation-skipping trusts."

After 1986, the amount of property that any individual may place in a generation-skipping trust is generally limited to $1,000,000. The trusts can even be drafted to "skip" more than one generation, and continue to be held in trust for a long period of time. However, Texas law places a maximum time limit on the duration of these types of trusts, which is referred to as the "perpetuities period." Generation-skipping trusts can usually last for several generations before the perpetuities period expires.

Any property passing to a generation-skipping trust that exceeds the limits on the amount of property placed in the trust will become subject to generation-skipping transfer taxes upon the beneficiary's death. These taxes are similar to estate taxes, but are automatically imposed upon property at the maximum estate tax bracket.

### Non-Tax Advantages of Trusts

Aside from the tax advantages of trusts previously described, there are numerous non-tax advantages. As noted, one of the most important of these is to provide for the proper management of the trust assets. For example, a person may feel that a loved one does not have the appropriate skills to properly invest funds they would otherwise receive outright. Therefore, the property can be placed in trust to be invested by a trusted relative, friend, business associate, or bank for the benefit of the beneficiary.

Second, the settlor may wish to give property to several beneficiaries, but the property requires management by only one or two persons. An example could be a small business or a ranch. The assets could be placed in trust for the benefit of a number of beneficiaries, but only one or two people would have the power to manage the assets as trustees. A trust in this instance would provide the advantages of spreading the economic benefits of the assets while centralizing the management of the assets.

A third non-tax advantage of a trust is the protection of assets from creditors of the beneficiary. Most trusts typically include a "spendthrift provision." A spendthrift provision prevents the beneficiary from either selling or mortgaging his or her interest in the trust. While they continue to receive distributions as provided in the trust instrument or at the trustees' discretion, the provision effectively prevents the beneficiary from losing his or her interest in the trust by making some other foolish investment decision. Similarly, the assets would remain as a "nest egg" in the event the beneficiary incurred some unforeseen tort liability, such as a large damage award against the beneficiary in an automobile wreck caused by the beneficiary. However, if a settlor retains any interest in property placed in trust, the spendthrift provision will be ineffective to protect the retained interest from the settlor's creditors.

### Summary

Irrevocable trusts, created either while living or by will, are extremely useful estate planning tools, both for tax and non-tax reasons. Large tax savings can be realized; but even more important, proper management of property and provisions for effective security for one's family often can be assured only through trusts.

# 19

# My Farm or Business

Many people have devoted their lives and energies to developing a successful business enterprise. This business operation may be a sole proprietorship, a partnership, or a closely held corporation. The business involved may include everything from farming to manufacturing. It may employ two persons or 2000. Whether the success of the individual who was the spark behind the business can survive his death will depend largely on the amount of planning that has been done for the protection of the business.

Most businessmen are so preoccupied with daily business problems that they fail to realize that all the benefits of their business may be lost to the family after death, unless proper preparations have been made for the orderly continuation or disposition of these business interests.

What are some of the basic problems which should be considered in planning the protection of the value of a one-man business at the time of the owner's death?

### Sale or Continued Operation

The first consideration that must be made after the business owner's death is whether to sell the business or continue its operations. This important decision will provide the framework for planning the protection of the surviving family.

Any business, regardless of its legal form, can become paralyzed following the death of its owner. Uninterrupted production during this period is usually difficult because the individual who has been responsible for the daily operations and decisions is gone. An orderly plan for the transfer of operational and managerial control or immediate sale is essential to insure the realization of maximum values for the owner's family.

A sole proprietorship is a business in which an individual usually owns all of the assets himself. If he dies, the executor of the estate will usually be under a duty to liquidate the business without delay to preserve the present value of the assets (unless provisions have been made in the will for the continuation of the business).

If the business is one in which the owner's personal services were the primary income producing factor, it is probably advisable to arrange for a sale of the business assets at his death. Care should be exercised in specifying which assets used in the business are to be sold, and some specific provisions should be made for payment of the business liabilities.

But if the business is one in which the owner's capital investment was the primary income producing factor, it is generally in the best interests of the family to arrange for a continuation of the business. This may be done by directing the executor of the will to continue the business and by providing him with broad powers to permit prompt action in exercising of sound business judgment. Alternatively, the will may direct that the business be operated in trust or be incorporated. It should provide for an immediate transfer and delivery of the business assets to insure continuity of operations.

A partnership is usually terminated on the death of a partner, and the surviving partners are required by law to liquidate the business and make an accounting to the deceased partner's estate. It is possible, by making appropriate provisions in the will, to continue the partnership operations with the decedent's estate or beneficiaries. The deceased partner's will should include specific directions with respect to the continuance or liquidation of the partnership.

Partnership agreements can be drawn to protect the deceased partner's interest from forced sale or involuntary liquidation. The partners should decide during their lifetimes whether to sell their interests at death or provide for the continued participation of their families. The decision to sell or continue the business operations upon the death of a partner should be incorporated into the partnership agreement and each partner's will in order to protect both the surviving partner, or partners, and the decedent's family.

The ownership of a corporate business enterprise by an individual is evidenced by stock ownership. The decision of sale or continued operation of a decedent's corporation is complex. The general considerations in selling a sole proprietorship are equally applicable here. If personal services are a major factor, a sale at death is desirable while the business should be continued if a capital investment is a major factor. In addition it is necessary to consider other factors.

The ownership of all the stock in a business corporation frequently represents a substantial part of the total value of the decedent's estate. This creates problems both as to its sale and its retention, which are probably best resolved in light of the surrounding circumstances and existing business conditions at the time of the owner's death.

Hence, the executor under the will should be given discretionary powers to participate in the management and operations of the corporate business. The executor or a trustee of a testamentary trust may be given specific instructions in the will on how and when to sell the stock, whom to sell it to, and when and under what circumstances it should be sold and liquidated. These directions may be given to the best advantage by the owner, in light of his experience and judgment in the business operations, and will provide valuable guidelines to protect his business after his death.

## The Federal Estate Tax and State Inheritance Taxes

The next consideration in protecting the value of a business after its owner's death is the federal income and estate tax assessments and state inheritance tax.

Once the decision has been made to sell or retain the owner's business, an estate plan can be formulated to minimize the various federal and states taxes triggered by death and imposed upon the subsequent transfer and receipt of property.

Federal estate taxes and state inheritance taxes can be avoided at the death of the first spouse where a husband and wife have properly structured their wills. Congress, through the use of the marital deduction, views a husband and wife as a single taxpayer for purposes of the estate tax as long as the first spouse to die leaves his or her property to the surviving spouse. Thus, property left to a surviving spouse will not be taxed for transfer tax purposes until the death of the surviving spouse. Property planning can, therefore, mean the difference between incurring a substantial tax when the first spouse dies or no tax. Eliminating the transfer tax can also mean fewer difficulties with which to contend in transferring the business.

## *Liquidity*

Death creates a need for cash. Many businessmen operate on credit for extensive periods of time and are constantly rearranging their business financing to provide working capital for their personal needs. This source of cash usually ends upon the businessman's death. Yet funds must be provided for the family's living expenses, as well as for the decedent's debts and the various taxes involved.

If the business or its assets is to be sold, the terms of the sale should be framed to insure the availability of funds for these taxes. If the business is to be continued at death, the owner's estate and business planning must provide the funds necessary to pay the taxes which are levied on the value of an individual's taxable estate.

In a sole proprietorship this may be accomplished by providing for the sale of specific assets for cash, by providing life insurance for the estate, or by providing the executor with appropriate directions and powers to borrow the necessary funds.

In a partnership agreement provisions for funds to pay taxes may be made by providing for withdrawals from the deceased partner's capital account. Current partnership earnings could also be provided for a period after death for this purpose. It is important to designate these payments as a continuation of income participation by the deceased partner's estate, so that such payments could not be mistaken for payments in purchase of the decedent's interest. Also, some funding arrangement may be incorporated in the partnership agreement which will specify and provide the source of funds to be used to purchase the decedent's interest or to provide money with which continued operations may be financed during this difficult transition period.

Naturally, the owners of a closely held corporation may experience great difficulty in raising cash because of the limited market for the securities. However, under certain conditions the law permits the corporation to redeem some of the stock in order to pay funeral expenses, death taxes, and other costs involved in administering the decedent's estate. This means that the corporate business operations can be used to provide the case funds needed, but before this is done a study should be made to determine if there are any adverse income tax consequences in such a redemption. This privilege of stock redemption is one that should be carefully studied in the estate plan, as it provides many opportunities for preserving the value of a corporate business for the survivors.

## Buy-Sell Agreements

Planning the continuation of any business after the death of its owner may be accomplished through a buy-sell agreement. This agreement is a contract which provides for the purchase and sale of the business interest, whether a sole proprietorship, partnership, or corporation.

The contract may be used to insure that interested and qualified individuals purchase the business under terms and conditions which recognize the full values involved, and which protect the surviving family from forced sales and depressed prices.

Buy-sell agreements may include provisions for funding the purchase price and assuring that the cash will be available to the decedent's estate. These provisions may be as broad and varied as the imagination of the business planner, but they should have one main purpose—the protection for the benefit of his surviving family of the business value created by the individual during his lifetime.

## Community Property

Texas community property law has already been discussed in detail. However, it should be remembered that if the business operation is community property, the death of the wife can create financial problems similar to those created upon the death of the husband. This is because the wife owns half of the business under Texas community property laws.

It is, therefore, necessary to consider all of the generalizations set forth in the foregoing discussion as they relate to the financial needs of the husband upon the wife's death. Failure to recognize that the death of the wife in a community property state can create all of the cash problems created at the death of the husband will produce serious consequences.

Each businessman should see that his wife's share of the community property is protected in the event she dies first. This will involve having her estate planned in the same basic program which is developed to protect the value of the business should he die first.

### Preserving the Family Farm

Congress has recognized the importance of the family farm in providing a relief provision in the estate tax laws dealing with the valuation of such farms for purposes of the federal transfer tax. Rather than valuing the family farm at the highest and best use value, the relief provision allows a lower special use value which results in less estate tax. To avail the estate for such favorable relief, however, Congress requires that the farm remain a "family farm," i.e., the individuals inheriting the farm must be family members only. Other technical rules must be complied with and therefore individuals interested in passing the family farm down through the generations should plan now to qualify for the special use value.

### Summary

There are no cure-all substitutes for thorough business planning to preserve the value of a farm or business at the time of the owner's death. Nor is there a device by which all problems created at death can be easily resolved.

A well considered plan which studies each of the problems peculiar to the business operation of the individual is essential, in order to preserve and protect the value of this business at the owner's death.

# 20

# Time Schedule for Estate Administration

The time required to have a will probated, or to have an estate administered by the probate court if there is no will, is often given as an argument against permitting an estate to go through probate. Actually, Texas probate procedure is time consuming only if the particular circumstances warrant it. The federal income and estate tax laws often make it advantageous for the estate to be kept open as long as possible. For example, it could be disadvantageous to close and distribute an estate immediately if having the estate as a separate income taxpayer will divide income between two or more taxpayers and result in lower income taxes because of taxation at lower rate brackets. The estate may also need to be kept open to afford time to accumulate funds to pay estate taxes.

Other factors may make a longer period of administration necessary. A poorly planned or drawn will may require a court action before it can be understood. Certain real property title transfers from the estate and handling the decedent's business interests at death simply cannot be disposed of overnight. A lifetime transfer to a living trust will not avoid most of these problems and, instead, may prevent the use of helpful tax-saving techniques.

### *The Texas Independent Executor*

What is involved in Texas probate and administration? A Texas independent executor, operating under a simplified procedure, has important duties, some of which must be performed whether or not the decedent has used a living trust.

When a Texas resident dies, the executor named in the will sees that burial instructions in the will or in a letter to the executor or funeral home are properly carried out even before the will is probated. He looks after unprotected properties such as securities, cash, jewelry, and perishable assets. He determines whether there is adequate insurance against loss. He confers with the heirs, finds out whether the surviving spouse has sufficient funds to meet current living expenses, whether there is a bank or savings account to which the survivor can have interim access, and whether any other problems need immediate attention. He helps with the proof of death for insurance purposes and generally prepares to collect the assets of the estate, which will be his responsibility when the will is probated.

Next, the executor must locate the will and have an attorney file it for probate. After notice is given to all interested persons by posting at the courthouse, the executor obtains a certificate of authority from the probate court (letters testamentary) to act as executor of the will. The executor then begins the task of finding out what the estate consists of. He must locate all bank and savings accounts and transfer them to a proper account in the name of the estate. He must identify and determine the terms of all certificates of deposit. He obtains custody of securities, which may or may not be transferred into his name as executor, depending on how long the estate will be in administration. He must assume authority over any business owned by the estate, and make arrangements for its management, protection, and continuance so that, if possible, no loss of value or personnel will occur. He must locate and actually or symbolically take possession of all other assets of the estate. He must determine the precise legal title to all property in order to be sure that the property he finds is legally a part of the probate estate he will administer, as well as determine the will's effect on those assets. The executor must keep detailed records of all his actions.

He must not let estate property get mixed with his own property or with the property of any other person. If the decedent leaves a surviving spouse, the executor must separate and clearly define the half of the community property belonging to the surviving spouse. He must segregate the separate property of the decedent from that of the survivor and from the survivor's share of the community property. There may be problems with assets that are located in different states or even in foreign countries. He must collect all the money owed the estate. He has power to compromise, abandon, or sue for collection of any claim that the estate has and must take appropriate and timely action on all claims.

A detailed, sworn inventory of estate assets must be made and filed with the court within 90 days of the appointment of the executor unless the court grants an extension of time. Assets must be designated as community or separate property and their value must be determined. This will be necessary also for state inheritance and federal estate tax use if the estate will incur these taxes. Whether to request the court to appoint appraisers to assist him in determining the value of the property is a matter of discretion based on the nature of the assets. Any interested person can ask the court to appoint appraisers if the executor does not. The executor must estimate how much cash is needed to pay funeral bills, medical bills, and current bills, as well as debts, taxes, and administration expenses. He must provide for any specific cash legacies in the will. If it is necessary to liquidate any assets to provide funds for payment of debts and cash gifts, the executor must see to that. Here he must determine the advisability of sales as opposed to retention of assets for future family use and then arrange and conduct any necessary sales. Usually, a purchaser of an estate asset will require that the executor secure a waiver of the federal estate tax lien.

The executor must properly estimate, provide for, and pay the income taxes that will be due for the portion of the year that had elapsed prior to the decedent's death. He must also take care of the estate's income taxes because the estate is a separate income taxpayer, and he must plan for and pay any federal estate tax and Texas inheritance tax.

He must receive income as it comes in, and he should watch investments so that appropriate action can be taken to protect estate values. If, for example, the price of a stock held by the estate is going down, the executor must decide whether it should be sold in favor of a more promising asset. A proper will provision makes this task easier.

At the end of the period of administration he must distribute the estate in accordance with the will. He must determine the timing of distributions to beneficiaries with a view toward the most advantageous income tax effect. Here, he must take account of and reconcile as far as reasonably possible any conflicts of interest that arise among the several beneficiaries. If the will calls for the setting up of trusts, he must determine when and to what extent trusts are to be set up, as well as determining which assets should be used to fund the trusts. Handling this properly can mean important tax savings.

After he has made all proper disbursements and distributed the estate, the period of his administration is over.

### Dependent Administration

An administrator—a person appointed by the court when there is no will or when the executor named is unable to act—acts in the same capacity as an executor would. Unless the court and all beneficiaries of the estate agree that it is in the best interests of the estate to have an independent administrator, the administrator will be dependent, meaning that he or she acts under the supervision of the court and must obtain court authorization before taking most actions in the administration of the estate. Compared with independent administration, dependent administration is more time consuming because it is necessary to notify the court of most actions taken. There are statutory waiting periods between applying for court approval of an action, getting court permission to act, filing a report to the court on the action taken, and, in the case of a sale of property, obtaining an order confirming the sale. Although these periods provide protection against hasty action, they also use up time.

Another time-consuming step in administering the estate of an intestate decedent is the court procedure for determining who his heirs are.

### Time Sequence of Administration

#### Proving the Will

With this brief outline of the duties of an executor or a court-appointed administrator in mind, one may more easily understand a timetable of the events of probate. In the typical case, the family will make an effort to locate a will immediately after death in case it contains specific instructions dealing with burial. On rare occasions, the will contains bequests of organs of the body, although a Texas driver's license notation is much more likely to be effective for that purpose. If there are such instructions, they must be carried out at once. The will is then delivered to the lawyer, who files it in court promptly for probate.

Collecting the necessary names, addresses, and ages of persons named in the will and persons who are the decedent's heirs if he died without a will may cause some delay at this point. Facts concerning the decedent (date of death, age, marital history, children's birthdays) are generally readily available.

Notice of the filing of the application for probate is given to all persons concerned by posting it for 10 days on the notice board at the county courthouse. If posting is done by a Thursday, the probate hearing may be held the second Monday after the posting, or any time thereafter. Usually, within the week after that Monday, if the will is not contested, a brief hearing occurs. It is proved to the court that the decedent is dead, that he lived or had property within the county, that four years have not elapsed since his death, and that the will was properly executed and witnessed according to Texas law. The court then enters an order probating (proving) the will. At the same time, or immediately thereafter, the executor named in the will or the administrator appointed by the court executes his oath to perform his duties as such, and the period of administration begins.

The total elapsed time to this point is two to three weeks, depending on how quickly the initial information was assembled. Most wills are self-proved in Texas. In such a case, there is no necessity for the time-consuming process of searching for the witnesses to the will to prove its proper execution. Self-proof provides this necessary element of proving proper execution without the witnesses testifying in court, provided no contention is raised at the court hearing that the testator was incompetent or unduly influenced when the will was made.

*Collecting and Valuing Property*

Immediately after qualifying, the executor or administrator begins the process of collecting and identifying the assets and determining their respective values. The time involved here depends on the nature and complexity of the estate and the availablity and completeness of accounting and other property records. If there are few assets and no claims of consequence, the process of identifying the assets is simple. Valuation for tax purposes may or may not consume an appreciable amount of time, depending on the kind and quantity of the assets involved and whether an appraisal is necessary. If the assets are personal property (household furniture, jewelry, and the like), the period of valuation is relatively short. Essentially, the time element depends on how soon the appraisers can fit an appraisal into their schedules. Usually, only a week or two are involved in this process. Real estate appraisals, on the other hand, generally take longer, partly because the number of persons qualified and available to do real estate appraisals is relatively small, and it takes longer for one of these appraisers to find time to examine the property and make the actual appraisal. Some pieces of real estate of relatively small value may be valued on the basis of estimates by informed persons without formal appraisal. The more numerous or sizeable or unique the pieces of real estate, the more time is required for fair and reasonable evaluation.

Understanding the process of real estate appraisal also aids understanding the time requirements. Properties in the same general category will have generally the same characteristics, so the appraiser may arrive at the value of an estate property by considering recent sales of other, comparable properties in the area. Sound evaluation requires that such real estate information be assembled, sorted, and assessed. Although no sale of the estate property is contemplated, it is necessary to establish the fair market value of that property. One must answer a hypothetical question: What would a buyer have been willing to pay a seller who was willing to sell on the date of the decedent's death? While the answer is a matter of opinion, it should have some rational basis that can be documented and made part of the appraisal.

Another kind of property that requires time to value is closely held stock. Valuation of listed stock is simple since immediately available market quotations show comparable sales. In contrast, a family corporation or a partnership in which there may not have been a sale for many years, and in which sales that have occurred may not be representative because of special surrounding circumstances, presents a much more complex problem. A sole proprietorship presents similar problems in locating and identifying sales of similar businesses. Every closely held business is unique, and this uniqueness must be sought out and then, if necessary, demonstrated to the taxing authorities. In all these cases, valuation takes time.

Much time can be saved for an executor by a testator's careful preparation for this valuation process. If he leaves a detailed list of assets, accompanied by much of the necessary data for appraisal purposes as well as data showing original cost and the cost of subsequent improvements, his executor's or administrator's job is simplified and shortened.

*Paying Creditor Claims*

An independent executor moves at his own speed after he has satisfied the requirement of preparing and filing an inventory of the estate. He should set aside the homestead and the tax exempt personal property or allowances in lieu of them, and provide the family allowance for the surviving spouse and minor children, if applicable. He may take a reasonable time to pay claims against the estate. If the claims are few and uncomplicated, payment can be made rapidly and the estate readied for distribution to the beneficiaries. If litigation arises, or if claims are disputed, an independent executor has adequate opportunity to dispose of these matters in the sensible, normal way that the testator could have done had he lived. Handling creditors' claims in a dependent administration takes more time because, for each step, the executor or administrator must apply to the court for permission, report his performance to the court, and secure the court's final approval for his action. The obvious consequence is that in dependent administration the proceedings are prolonged.

The executor or adminstrator must, within 30 days after his or her appointment, publish a notice to creditors that they should submit their claims against the estate, and must, within four months after his or her appointment, give notice by certified or registered mail to certain secured and unsecured creditors. The claims of creditors should be presented within six months from the date of death. Ordinarily, however, creditors' claims are not formally filed. The handling of debts in an estate is usually no problem. Current expenses, such as costs of the last illness, are paid in cash long before any necessity for filing a claim arises. Those who hold mortgage debts also usually continue to look to the security and file no claims.

Still, the procedure for presenting or filing claims exists, and the possibility of such claims, although their existence may be unknown, is another reason estates are often kept open by an independent executor for at least six months. If a plan of early distribution of the estate based on known claims is followed, the executor and the distributees run the risk that after all funds have been distributed (and perhaps spent) they will be faced by a claim that they are unable to satisfy. Should the executor be prepared to take such a risk, then the estate may be effectively closed and distributed as soon as the inventory is filed. In fact, this risk is often taken, and the handling of debts presents no more of a problem than during one's lifetime. After completing administration, an executor may choose not to take the final step of formally closing the estate, because formal closing deprives him of authority to handle any future matter that might arise unexpectedly, such as discovering a previously unknown estate asset.

## Accounting and Distribution

As soon as taxes and debts have been provided for, the executor is ready to make distribution to the beneficiaries under the will. Unlike an executor or administrator in a dependent administration, an independent executor has no duty to make any final accounting, unless his actions are challenged by a beneficiary. He may at this time file an affidavit in court that all debts and taxes have been paid. It is wise to draw up a distribution statement for the information of the beneficiaries and proceed to make a distribution based upon it. Depending on the nature of the assets, the terms of the will, the identity and financial circumstances of the beneficiaries, and any resulting conflicts of interest among them, the executor will work to reconcile differences and make the most beneficial asset distribution.

Once the asset allocation is determined, actually preparing the distribution statement and making the necessary distribution is essentially a paper-work chore. Where there is no conflict among the beneficiaries and all are aware of the respective interests, such a distribution list may be unnecessary. If adequate accounting records are maintained, they may suffice. However, an executor or administrator in a dependent administration must prepare a formal final account to be filed with the court. Notice must be given to the heirs along with the opportunity to question the account, and a court order must be obtained approving the account and directing the distribution. Then follows the distribution itself, a report to the court that the distribution has been made, and an order from the court approving the report and discharging the administrator or executor.

Despite the number of tasks involved, the process moves rapidly. Some estates are closed within six months or less. A longer time span usually results when death taxes are involved, or when determination of heirship is difficult.

After an estate has been in independent administration for fifteen months, a person with an interest in the estate may demand an accounting by the executor. After two years of independent administration, a person with an interest in the estate may seek a court order compelling the executor to close the estate and distribute its assets.

*Federal Estate Tax*

The chief reason for a lengthy probate administration is the nature of federal tax law.

If an estate is large enough to incur federal estate tax, a federal estate tax return has to be filed within nine months after the date of death. This extended period stems from the fact that federal tax law permits an estate to be valued either as of the date of death or as of six months after the date of death, with the executor having the option of paying tax at the lower of the two values, an option first granted during the depression of the 1930s. It is desirable, where a federal estate tax may be due and a tax saving is possible, to delay winding up the estate until it can be valued six months from the date of death. Thus, for the protection of the estate, the appraisals mentioned previously have to be made twice; once as of the date of death and again as of six months later. Little, if any, extra time or expense of the appraisers is required for making the second valuation, since most of the work will have been done in the date-of-death appraisal.

The executor will usually find it wiser to postpone paying estate tax until it is due, giving the estate the benefit of the use of the money as long as possible. If the estate consists in large part of a closely held business, installment payment of the estate tax over a number of years is permitted. This allows time for assets to be sold at other than distress prices, and for funds to be accumulated from income to avoid sales of property that should be retained for the family. Timing in these cases, though it involves delay in distribution, works to the benefit of the heirs.

*Income Tax*

The federal income tax sometimes prompts an even longer extension of the administration period. For federal income tax purposes, the estate—which comes into being at the moment of death—is a separate tax-payer with a separate exemption and a separate applicable tax bracket. During the period that the estate exists, it provides a separate pocket into which income may be placed and on which federal income tax is payable at a bracket that may be lower than for the beneficiaries. Either the estate or the beneficiaries pay income tax on an item of income received by the estate, but not both. If the tax bracket applicable to the beneficiaries is higher than that applicable to the estate, it will benefit the beneficiaries to maintain the estate as a taxpayer for as long as permissible under federal law.

Estates that remain open from two to five years or more are probably kept open mainly for federal tax reasons rather than delinquency, procrastination, or mismanagement on the part of lawyers, judges, executors, or appraisers. The simple truth is that an executor who does his job thoroughly will not close the estate so long as it is in the best interest of the beneficiaries to keep it open, assuming that he operates within the permissible rules laid down by the Internal Revenue Service and by the courts. The testator's and subsequently the executor's planning and judgment will determine whether keeping the estate open for a substantial period is of advantage to the beneficiaries.

In the final analysis, if a will is properly drawn and names an independent executor, the paper-work steps will not be the time-consuming factor. Federal taxation will be behind any real delay.

### Comparison with a Living Trust

A living trust (discussed in Chapter 15) may simplify the problem of passing on certain assets. If the trust is properly set up in the beginning, some of the valuation and organization of assets will have been done at that time. It will only be necessary to bring them up to date at the time of death. An individual trustee, however, may not have carefully evaluated and assembled the assets, and there will be little or no time saved at death. But the assets of the trust must be listed and valued for federal estate and Texas inheritance tax purposes. The same valuation and tax procedures must be followed as if the trust had not been created. It makes little time difference that some trust assets may not appear as part of the probate inventory.

A living trust can actually result in increased expense. In one respect a living trust is definitely disadvantageous, since it prevents the executor from utilizing a combination of the estate and a testamentary trust (one created by the will) as separate federal-income-tax paying pockets. Although the estate is not large enough to incur estate tax, the income tax savings under a properly drawn will may well justify passing of income from estate to testamentary trust to beneficiary. The amounts saved in any one year may not be large in themselves, but they can be substantial over an extended period, for example, from a beneficiary's infancy to age 18. The few dollars saved each year can add to a child's enjoyment during the years of his education and growth to maturity. In a large estate the presence of this extra tax pocket during the period of estate administration can justify the extra expense and time that may result from choosing a testamentary trust over a revocable living trust.

Estate administration through probate is not significantly more time consuming than through a living trust. A living trust for all property of the decedent has its uses, but its virtues can be outweighed by the loss of important tax advantages to be gained by passing the entire estate through administration by a Texas independent executor.

# 21

# What Will Probate Cost?

Of universal interest is the question, "What will probate cost my estate?" The answer involves careful consideration of the size, type, and location of the present and future assets comprising the estate income, any tax complications present, the simplicity or complexity of the disposition of the estate, the extent and type of the debts, and various other factors.

This chapter will deal with costs and expenses in relatively routine administrations. It will not cover probate intricacies in unusual situations or complicated probate litigation involving appeals to or actions in the district court, the court of civil appeals, and the Supreme Court of Texas. Such actions lack broad application.

### Court Cost and Bond Premiums—The Well-Drawn Will

Court costs are set out in the state law (Texas Local Government Code §118.001 et seq.) and in schedules of charges published by the clerks responsible for handling the court papers. Such costs may include a small fee to cover a wide variety of court services for one year from the filing of an application to probate a will or for administration of an estate. In addition, there may be other costs, such as minimal charges for filing and entering a claim against the estate and after the first year of administration, a charge for filing and recording a legal document, and so on. The lawyer can make an accurate estimate of court costs once he knows whether there is provision for an independent executor, whether bond has been waived, the nature and extent of the decedent's assets, whether there is a probability of litigation, and similar facts.

Court costs can be reduced to a minimum by naming an independent executor without bond. With such a provision in the will, there will be only a small filing fee, because no court costs would accrue after probating the will and obtaining letters testamentary. Without the independent administration in a will, greater costs will be incurred. For example, various filing of claims by creditors would entail extra costs.

If not waived by the will, any person appointed executor or administrator must post bond in an amount equal to the estimated value of the estate (excluding real estate) and an additional amount equal to one year's expected estate revenue from all sources. This includes interest, dividends, periodical payments, and rentals for use of real and personal property and so on.

## Appraiser Fees

Under the Texas Probate Code, provision is made for the appointment by the probate court of "disinterested" persons to appraise the property of the estate to be administered. Each appraiser is entitled by law to receive a minimum compensation of $5 per day for each day of actual service in the performance of his duties.

## Executor's or Administrator's Fees

The fee of the executor or the administrator is set by law. Under the Texas Probate Code (Section 241) and in the absence of a contrary direction by the decedent's will, executors and administrators are entitled to receive a commission of 5 percent on all amounts they actually receive in cash, and a commission of 5 percent on all amounts actually paid out by them in cash during the administration of the estate. No commission is allowed for cash belonging to the decedent on hand or on deposit at the time of his death, nor for paying out cash to the heirs or legatees.

Such commission is subject to a limitation that in no event shall the executor or administrator receive in the aggregate more than 5 percent of the gross fair market value of the estate subject to administration. It is further provided that "If the executor or administrator manages a farm, ranch, factory, or other business of the estate, or if the compensation as calculated above is unreasonably low," the court is authorized to allow him "reasonable compensation" for his services, and for such purpose the county court can act upon applications from independent executors.

A testator can direct that his executor receive no compensation, or a fixed dollar amount which may be less than the statutory amount. If the executor agrees to serve under those conditions, he is bound by them. Of course it would be unreasonable in most situations to ask anyone other than a beneficiary under the will to serve without compensation.

### Attorneys' Fees Are Not Set by Law

Texas, unlike other states, does not set the amount of the attorney's fee but provides that the fee shall be "reasonable." The attorney's fee is regarded as a private matter to be agreed upon between the lawyer and client in accordance with proper standards of reasonableness.

If an administration is under probate court control, the attorney must prove the reasonableness of his fee to the court. This is usually done by witnesses who from their experience and knowledge are familiar with the value of services and advice rendered by lawyers in probate matters.

### Percentage of the Estate

One method of determining a proper fee for probate services is by applying a small percentage figure to the total value of the property subject to probate or taxation. Such a percentage figure is useful in making an estimate of the attorney's fee prior to the service when specific facts concerning the estate are not available.

The attorney's fee includes all usual and customary work done by him up to and through the approval of the inventory, the issuance of notice to creditors, and the tax settlement. Such services include attending conferences; consulting and advising prior to probate; preparing an application for probate; attending court to probate the will and obtain letters testamentary or letters of administration; advising and consulting the executor or administrator during administration; giving opinions on will interpretation, payment of claims, handling of the estate assets, and partition and distribution; preparing federal estate and state inheritance tax returns; and supervising the audit and approving tax returns. In the administration of estates under court control the attorney's fee will include extraordinary or unusual services and those in connection with applications, orders, and accounts in the course of administration which might be necessary to obtain court approval to sell or lease assets or do other things required in administrations under court control. In such cases it will also include the preparation and filing of annual and final accounts for the executor or administrator and obtaining court approval. Charges for such matters are based on the time and difficulty of the service and the values involved. Where complicated tax accounting and reporting is necessary, an additional reasonable charge is made.

### Determining Reasonableness of Attorneys' Fees

The Model Rules of Professional Conduct promulgated by the American Bar Association in 1983 provide that a lawyer's fee shall be reasonable, and that the relevant factors in determining the reasonableness of a fee include the following:

1. The time and labor required, the novelty and difficulty of the questions involved, and the skill requisite to perform the legal service properly.
2. The likelihood, if apparent to the client, that the acceptance of the particular employment will preclude other employment by the lawyer.
3. The fee customarily charged in the locality for similar legal services.
4. The amount involved and the results obtained.
5. The time limitations imposed by the client or by the circumstances.
6. The nature and length of the professional relationship with the client.
7. The experience, reputation, and ability of the lawyer or lawyers performing the services.
8. Whether the fee is fixed or contingent.

No one of these considerations in itself is controlling. They are guides in ascertaining the real value of the service. After the attorney's services and advices have been rendered to an estate, the suggested percentage fee may be inappropriate in the light of these considerations. The responsible attorney will adjust his fee accordingly, making an increase or reduction according to services rendered. In many, if not most estates, if the attorney has actively and fully discharged his obligation to the estate, the percentage figure is a fairly reliable guide in setting the fee, particularly if the fee was not set prior to performance of the legal service.

If a reputable attorney is employed on a reasonable fee basis and allowed to await the completion of his services before setting his fee, he will not overstate the value of such services nor demand a fee which is unreasonable.

### *Trust Administration*

The costs relating to trust administration are not properly included as probate costs. Trust services vary widely depending upon their exact nature as specified in the trust instrument. Where a trust is created under a will, the trustee takes over the trust administration upon the termination of the administration and delivery of the trust assets by the executor. The trust also can be created during a grantor's lifetime by delivery of the trust assets directly to the trustee in a trust agreement.

In the absence of such an understanding, the testator can designate the amount of the trustee's compensation, subject only to the willingness of the trustee to serve for such an amount. This can be based on a percentage of the fair market value of the trust property or on a certain percent of the gross income of the trust estate each year. If there are co-trustees, it can be provided that one (usually the individual trustee) shall receive no compensation, but that the other (usually the corporate trustee) shall receive reasonable compensation. The possibilities for different compensation arrangements are quite varied.

### *What Will a Will Cost?*

The cost of a will is small, considering how much knowledge, experience, and skill are necessary to produce it. For the preparation of a simple will, one giving all the property outright to one or more persons with provisions for independent executor without bond, a minimum of $125 may be charged. Where the will is more complicated, such as one creating a testamentary trust providing for one or more life estates or setting forth lengthy or complicated testamentary provisions, the fee may be a minimum of $175, the same figure as for the preparation of a trust established by a living person during his lifetime.

Where a wife's will is to contain substantially the same provisions as her husband's, the charge may be only half the charge for the husband's will.

All of the foregoing are possible minimum fees. Various complexities and complications requiring additional services and advice will suggest additional fees in instances where greater efforts and knowledge are required than in routine drafting.

If a person requires the services of an attorney in preparing a will, he should not be hesitant to inquire about the legal expense. It should be discussed frankly so that reasonable arrangements can be made in advance of the preparation of the will. If extensive estate planning services are required in addition to the drafting of instruments, ordinarily the fee for such services will be based upon the time actually spent in such services.

## *Summary*

Texas had led the way among American jurisdictions in streamlining its probate procedures to minimize probate costs and simplify the administration of decedents' estates by dispensing with formal court administration. With a proper will probate court costs are minimal, and there is no bonding expense. The fees of executors and administrators can be estimated once the gross value and nature of the estate and probable income and disbursements are known.

In Texas, attorneys' fees for services to the executor or administrator are not set by law but are the subject of private agreement. If an attorney is required to set or estimate a fee in advance, he may suggest a small percentage figure based upon the estate's gross value. If an attorney is employed on a reasonable fee basis to be determined upon completion of his services, he may make a charge to an executor or administrator that will be less than an arbitrary percentage figure. Such fee must be reasonable in light of all relevant factors such as those set out in the American Bar Association Model Rules of Professional Conduct. The fees of attorneys serving administrators under court control are subject to the approval of the probate court, and the court requires the attorney to prove the reasonableness of his charge. When a testator does not make a proper will, the cost of administering his estate will be higher than if a properly prepared will has been made by an attorney who was naturally familiar with expense-cutting provisions, meaning of legal terms, consequences of legal principles, requirements for executing wills, and the necessity for definiteness.

A person needing the services of an attorney should not hesitate to discuss his fee or any other cost of probate with him. Substantial savings of probate costs can be effected by proper planning.

# Glossary

*adjusted gross estate:* used only for federal estate tax purposes. The adjusted gross estate is the value of the decedent's estate for federal tax purposes figured by subtracting funeral and administrative expenses, debts, taxes, and certain other items from the total value of the estate.

*administrator:* one appointed by the court to administer the estate of the decedent. His principal duties are to collect the properties of the estate, pay the debts of the decedent, and distribute the estate to the people entitled to it. An administrator is appointed if the decedent failed to appoint an executor in his will or died without a will. The feminine form of administrator is "administratrix."

*appreciation:* growth in the fair market value of the property. The term usually refers to an increase due to fluctuation in the market value of the property rather than changes in the property itself. Autonym: depreciation.

*beneficiary:* one for whose benefit a trust is created, or one to whom the proceeds of insurance are payable.

*commingling:* the placing together of property of various kinds. In Texas the term has special significance with respect to community property and refers to the mixing of one spouse's separate property with community property or with separate property of the other spouse.

*community property:* property acquired by either spouse during marriage, except by gift, will or inheritance. This is a property system based on the theory that marriage is a partnership. Texas is one of eight community property states.

*convenience account:* a bank account established by one person (a) in the name of himself and another person (b) for the purpose of allowing either person (a or b) to draw out money to be used for the benefit of the first person. A common example of such an account is the situation in which the first person is aged or ill and is unable to go to the bank to obtain funds, so the account is established to allow a second person to draw funds for the "convenience" of the other.

*court-made law:* law which is established by court decision rather than by the act of the legislature. This term applies to interpretations of statutes and theories set forth in court decisions.

*decedent:* a deceased person. The term refers either to one who dies leaving a will or to one who dies without a will.

*devise:* (noun) a gift of real estate which is made by the will of a deceased person; (verb) to give real estate by means of a will.

*devisee:* one who receives real estate under the terms of a will.

*disposition:* transmitting or directing property ownership, as in disposition of property by a person's will.

*encumberance:* a claim, lien, charge, or liability against property, such as a mortgage.

*estate:* the entire property owned by a person, whether land or movable property. In the probate context the term refers to all property left by a decedent.

*executor:* one who is appointed in the will of a decedent to manage the estate and to carry out the directions in the will for disposition of the estate property. In Texas the testator can direct that his executor be independent of the control of the probate court. If he does not do so, then the executor acts only upon the order of the probate court. The feminine of executor is "executrix."

*fair market value:* the value of property that would be set by an owner willing (but not forced) to sell for cash and a buyer willing (but not forced) to buy for cash, with both buyer and seller knowing all relevant facts. The fair market value of property is intended to be an estimate of value which is fair, economic, and reasonable under normal conditions.

*grantor:* a person who transfers property, other than by will (where he would be called "testator") or trust (where he wold be called "settlor"), to someone else (known as the "grantee"). The term is generally used to describe the one who transfers property by gift or by sale.

*holographic will:* a will written entirely in the handwriting of the testator.

*intestate:* a person is said to die intestate when he leaves no valid will to control the disposition of his property.

*joinder:* joining or coupling together; uniting with another person in some legal step or proceeding.

*joint tenancy with right of survivorship:* generally, ownership of property by two or more persons who have the same interest in the property and own it together; all rights in the property pass to the survivor upon the death of anyone joint tenant and ultimately pass to the last survivor. Thus, the interest of a joint tenant is not included in his estate when he dies, since he cannot control the disposition of his interest in the property.

*letters testamentary:* a document of authority issued to an executor by the probate court showing his authority to serve as executor.

*liquidity:* used to describe whether an asset can be converted into cash easily. For example, stock which can be easily sold has good liquidity; stock which cannot be easily sold has poor liquidity.

*personalty:* property other than real estate is said to "personalty." The term also applies to contract rights.

*posting:* giving public notice, generally by displaying a written announcement in an official, conspicuous place attaching a notice to the courthouse bulletin board.

*probate:* the procedure for proving to the satisfaction of the probate court that an instrument is the last will and testament of the decedent.

*quitclaim deed:* the deed intended to transfer whatever interest the grantor had, if he had any at all. This deed is distinguished from a warranty deed, in which the grantor guarantees that he does have a certain interest.

*realty:* land and mineral interests. This includes buildings located on the land as well as crops and trees growing on the land. Synonyms: real estate, real property, or immovables.

*self-proving will:* a will which does not require that the witnesses appear in court to prove that the will was properly signed by the testator, because after signing the will the testator and the witnesses signed an additional document (not part of the will) in which they swear before a notary public that the will was correctly signed.

*separate property:* property owned by either spouse before marriage or property received by gift, under a will, or through inheritance during marriage.

*survivorship account:* a bank account in the name of two or more persons in which the entire amount passes to the survivor or survivors upon the death of one of the owners. The account may be with a company other than a bank.

*tenants in common:* ownership by two or more persons of the same piece of property in which each has the right to use and occupy the property at the same time with all the other owners. This type of ownership differs from the "joint tenancy with right of survivorship," in that the interest of the deceased owner does not pass to the survivors. Thus, a tenant in common may dispose of his interest by will.

*testator:* one who has made a will; one who dies leaving a will. The feminine of testator is "testatrix."

*trust:* a legal arrangement whereby property is transferred to one person for the benefit of another person.

*trustee:* the person who holds the property in trust for the benefit of another person who is called the beneficiary.

*valuation:* the act of ascertaining or estimating the worth of the property.

# About the Authors

**Lise E. Anderson, Dallas**

Born July 23, 1956, in Fort Worth, Texas. Admitted to the bar, 1981, Texas; 1987, Tennessee. University of Texas at Arlington (B.A. with highest honors, 1978), University of Texas (J.D., with honors, 1981). Organizations: Order of the Coif. Member: Dallas Bar Association; Sections of Taxation and Probate, State Bar of Texas; Sections of Taxation and Real Property, Probate and Trust Law, American Bar Association; Dallas Estate Planning Council. Areas of Practice: Exempt Organizations, Charitable Gift Planning, Estate Planning and Probate. Shareholder attorney: Johnson & Gibbs, Dallas, Texas.

**Thomas D. Anderson, Houston**

Born March 9, 1912, in Oklahoma City, Oklahoma. Admitted to bar, 1933, Virginia; 1934, Texas. Washington and Lee University (LL.B. 1934, J.D. 1969), Lambuth College (Honorary LL.D. 1967). U.S. Navy (commander, USNR), 1942–1946. Associated with Andrews & Kurth, and predecessor firms, 1934–1942, 1946–1947; Senior vice-president and trust officer, Texas Commerce Bank, Houston, and predecessor institutions, 1947–1956, 1960–1965. Member: Phi Delta Phi, Omicron Delta Kappa, State Bar of Texas, Houston Bar Association; Fellow: Texas Bar Foundation. Of counsel: Anderson, Brown, and Jones, Houston.

**Arthur H. Bayern, San Antonio**

Born January 28, 1934, in Bayside, New York. Admitted to bar, 1965, Texas. Colgate University (A.B. 1954), University of Texas School of Law (LL.B. 1965). Chairman, Real Estate, Probate and Trust Law Section, State Bar of Texas, 1981–1982; Chairman, A.B.A. Committee on Post-Mortem Estate and Tax Planning, 1979–1986;

President, San Antonio Estate Planners Council, 1972–1973; President, San Antonio Bar Association, 1980–1981; President, San Antonio Estate Planning and Probate Law Association, 1986–1987. Board Certified, Estate Planning and Probate Law, Texas Board of Legal Specialization; Fellow, American College of Trust and Estate Counsel. Principal: Bayern, Paterson, Aycock & Amen, P.C., San Antonio.

### John L. Bell, Jr., Beaumont

Born November 16, 1937, in Beaumont, Texas. Admitted to bar, 1962, Texas. University of Texas (B.B.A. 1960, LL.B. 1962). Fraternity: Phi Delta Phi. Author of articles in *Southwestern Law Journal* and *Baylor Law Review,* Coauthor of *Texas Estate Administration.* Member: Jefferson County Bar Association, State Bar of Texas, American Bar Association. Past chairman of the Section on Real Estate, Probate, and Trust Law of the State Bar of Texas. Fellow: American College of Trust and Estate Counsel. Member of the firm of Mehaffy & Webber, a Professional Corporation, Beaumont.

### Thomas E. Berry, Houston

Born July 26, 1923, in San Antonio, Texas. Admitted to bar, 1951, Texas. Southwestern University (B.B.A. 1944), University of Texas (B.B.A. 1949 LL.B. 1951). Fraternity: Phi Delta Phi. Member: Houston Bar Association, State Bar of Texas, American Bar Association. Member: Real Estate, Probate, and Trust Law Section of State Bar of Texas; Chairman, Committee on Estate Planning and Drafting: Irrevocable Trusts and Other Inter Vivos Trusts, ABA Real Property, Probate, and Trust Law Section; Chairman, Committee on Tax Practice Management, ABA Section of Taxation; Committee on Estate and Gift Tax ABA Tax Section; Member and past President Houston Business and Estate Planning Council; Member and past Director, Houston Estate & Financial Forum; Board Certified, Estate Planning and Probate Law, Texas Board of Legal Specialization; Fellow: American College of Trust and Estate Counsel. Member of the firm of Thomas E. Berry & Associates, Houston.

### Harvie Branscomb, Jr., Corpus Christi

Born March 24, 1922, in Dallas, Texas. Admitted to bar, 1958, Texas. Duke University (A.B. 1943), Yale University Law School (LL.B. 1948). Chairman, Tax Section, American Bar Association,

1980-1981; Member of American Law Institute; Member, American College of Tax Counsel; Member, American College of Trust and Estate Counsel; Trustee of the Southwestern Legal Foundation; Speaker at numerous institutes on federal taxation, and author of publications on federal tax subjects; certified public accountant. Partner: Matthews & Branscomb, Corpus Christi.

### James E. Brill, Houston

Born May 29, 1933 in Indianapolis, Indiana. Admitted to bar, 1957, Texas. The University of Texas (B.B.A. 1956; LL.B. 1957). Editor and Project Director, *The Texas Probate Systems* 1971-1992. Chairman, Law Practice Management Section, American Bar Association 1982-1983. President, State Junior Bar of Texas, 1968-1969. Chairman, Continuing Legal Education Committee, State Bar of Texas, 1975-1979. Fellow: American College of Trust and Estate Counsel, American Bar Foundation, Texas Bar Foundation. Presidents' Award, State Bar of Texas, 1978. Solo practitioner, Houston.

### Gordon R. Carpenter, Dallas

Born February 6, 1920, Denton, Texas. Admitted to bar, 1947, Texas. North Texas State University (B.S. 1940); Southern Methodist University School of Law (LL.B. 1948); Southwestern Legal Foundation (Exec. Sec. 1947-1956; Exec. Dir. 1956-1958); Southern Methodist University School of Law (Adm. Assistant to the Dean, 1951-1958). Chairman, Real Estate, Probate and Trust Law Section, State Bar of Texas, 1964-1965, and Chairman, CLE Committee, (1952-1954 and 1958-1966); President's Award 1963; Chairman, Texas Bankers Trust Division, 1980-1981; Life Fellow, Texas Bar Foundation, Vice President—Trust Officer, InterFirst Bank Dallas, 1958-1984.

### W. Fred Cameron, Houston

Born March 6, 1938, in Atlanta, Texas. Admitted to bar, 1962, Texas. Baylor University (B.B.A. 1960, J.D. 1962). Fellow, American College of Trust and Estate Counsel; Past Chairman of the Real Estate, Probate and Trust Law Section of the State Bar of Texas; Past Chairman, Estate Planning and Probate Advisory Commission of the Texas Board of Legal Specialization; Board Certified Specialist in Estate

Planning and Probate Law; listed in "The Best Lawyers in America"; Senior Partner and Co-Chairman of Trusts and Estates Department of Fulbright & Jaworski, Houston; Past-President of Houston Estate and Financial Forum, Baylor University Law Alumni Association and Baylor University Development Board; Regent of Baylor University.

### Harold A. Chamberlain, Houston

Born September 20, 1931, in East St. Louis, Illinois. Admitted to bar, 1957, Arkansas, 1963, Texas. Arkansas A&M (B.S. 1952); graduate study in finance, Auburn University; University of Arkansas School of Law (LL.B. 1957). Comments editor, *Arkansas Law Review.* Attorney for chief counsel's office, Internal Revenue Service, Dallas, 1957–1963; senior trial attorney, Tax Division, U.S. Department of Justice, 1961–1963. Member: Houston Bar Association, State Bar of Texas, American Bar Association. Fellow: Texas Bar Foundation.

### J. Chrys Dougherty, Austin

Born May 3, 1915, in Beeville, Texas. Admitted to bar, 1940, Texas. University of Texas (B.A. 1937); Harvard (LL.B. 1940); Chairman, Tax Section, State Bar of Texas, 1965–1966; President, State Bar of Texas, 1979–1980; Member, American College of Trust and Estate Counsel, 1976–; American College of Tax Counsel, 1983; International Academy of Estate and Trust Law, Texas State Bar College; Board Certified-Estate Planning and Probate Law and Tax Law, Texas Board of Legal Specialization; Contributing author: Bowe, "Estate Planning and Taxation," and "Texas Lawyers Practice Guide"; Fellow: American Bar, Texas Bar Foundations. Partner: Graves, Dougherty, Hearon & Moody, Austin. Assisted by S. Jody Helman.

### Joseph P. Hammond, El Paso

Born June 9, 1931, in Albuquerque, New Mexico. Admitted to bar, 1955, Texas. University of Texas (B.B.A. 1953, LL.B. 1955); Member: American Bar Association, State Bar of Texas, El Paso County Bar Association. Fellow: American College of Trust and Estate Counsel; Board Certified-Estate Planning & Probate Law, Texas Board of Legal Specialization; Council, Real Estate, Probate & Trust Law Section, State Bar of Texas (1982–1986). Lecturer and Chairman, University of Texas, El Paso Women's Estate Planning Seminar; Lecturer: Southwestern Legal Foundation (1977, 1979) State Bar of Texas Advanced Estate Planning Institute (1981, 1983). Shareholder, Kemp, Smith, Duncan and Hammond, El Paso.

### Allan Howeth, Fort Worth

Born February 19, 1938, Fort Worth, Texas. Admitted to bar, 1963, Texas. Texas Christian University (B.A. 1960). Southern Methodist University School of Law (J. D. Cum Laude 1963). Past Chairman of Real Estate, Probate and Trust Law Section of the State Bar of Texas. SMU Law School Executive Board. Board of Directors, State Bar of Texas (1988–91). Fellow, American College of Trust and Estate Counsel. Board certified, Estate Planning and Probate Law. Texas Board of Legal Specialization. Author, "Appointment and Qualification of Administrators and Executors," *Texas Estate Administration* (1975). Managing Partner, Cantey and Hanger, Fort Worth.

### H. David Hughes, Austin

Born March 7, 1947, Houston, Texas. Admitted to bar, 1972, Texas. University of Texas (B.B.A. 1969, J.D. 1971). Board Certified, Estate Planning and Probate Law, Texas Board of Legal Specialization. Fellow: The American College of Trust and Estate Counsel. Partner: Brown Maroney & Oaks Hartline, Austin. Member: Travis County and American Bar Associations; State Bar of Texas; Past-President Greater Houston Tax Forum; Chairman—State Bar of Texas Taxation Section on Committee on Inheritance Taxes, 1981–1983; member—State Bar of Texas Advanced Estate Planning and Probate Course Planning Committee, 1982. Speaker: State Bar of Texas Wills and Probate Practice Institute, 1975; The Southwestern Legal Foundation Institute on Wills and Probate, 1979; listed in "The Best Lawyers in America."

### Paul E. Martin, Houston

Born February 5, 1928, in Atchison, Kansas. Admitted to bar, 1956, Texas; 1958, Pennsylvania. Baylor University (B.A. 1955, LL.B.1956), Harvard University (LL.M. 1957). Fraternity: Phi Delta Phi. Houston Estate and Financial Forum (President, 1965–1966); member; Houston Business and Estate Planning Council; Board certified, Estate Planning and Probate Law, Texas Board of Legal Specialization; instructor in estate planning, University of Houston. Member:

Houston, American Bar Associations, State Bar of Texas. Fellow: American College of Trust and Estate Counsel. Senior Partner: Chamberlain, Hrdlicka, White, Williams & Martin, Houston.

### Lucian E. Morehead, Plainview
Born June 24, 1911, in Plainview, Texas. Admitted to bar, 1935, Texas. Wayland Baptist College, Baylor University (B.A. 1930); University of Texas (LL.B. 1935). Fraternities: Order of the Coif, Phi Delta Phi, Chancellors. Member: Texas Law Review Association. Chairman: Real Estate, Probate, and Trust Law Section, State Bar of Texas, 1968–1969; secretary-treasurer and editor of newsletter, 1966–1967; vice-chairman, 1967–1968. Fellow: American College of Trust and Estate Counsel; Charter and Sustaining Life Fellow: Texas Bar Foundation, Partner: Morehead & Tisdel, Plainview.

### C. Stephen Saunders, Austin
Born November 11, 1952, Houston, Texas. Admitted to the bar, 1980, Texas. The University of Texas at Austin (B.A. 1975, J.D. 1980). Fraternities: Phi Eta Sigma, Phi Beta Kappa. Member: Central Texas Estate Planning Council; Real Estate, Probate, and Trust Law Section, (Statutory Wills Committee), Section of Taxation (Exempt Organizations Subcommittee), State Bar of Texas; Real Property, Probate and Trust Law Section, American Bar Association. Member: Travis County, American Bar Associations, State Bar of Texas. Board Certified, Estate Planning and Probate Law. Shareholder: Jenkins & Gilchrist, A Professional Corporation, Austin.

### Edward B. Winn, Dallas
Born September 23, 1920, in Dallas, Texas. Admitted to bar, 1948, Texas. The University of Texas (B.A. 1942), Yale Law School (LL.B. 1948). President, State Junior Bar of Texas, 1953: president, Dallas Estate Council, 1954; chairman, Real Estate, Probate, and Trust Law Section, State Bar of Texas, 1962–1963; chairman, Real Property, Probate, and Trust Law Section, American Bar Association, 1963–1964; Chairman: Advisory Commission, Estate Planning and Probate Law, Texas Board of Legal Specialization, 1982 to present; chairman, Southwestern Legal Foundation Institute on Wills and Probate, 1965 to present. President, American College of Trust and Estate Counsel, 1974–1975. Member, Board of Governors, American Bar Association, 1985–1988, Partner: Winn, Beaudry & Virden, Dallas.

## C. B. Wheeler, Texarkana

Born December 5, 1916, in Texarkana, Texas. Admitted to bar, 1940, Texas; 1975, Arkansas; Texas A & M University, University of Texas (B.A. 1938, LL.B. 1940). Texas Law Review, Phi Delta Phi. Special Agent, FBI, 1941–1944; U.S. Marine Corps, 1944–1946. Chairman, Uniform State Laws Committee, 1965–1966; Chairman, Banking Laws Committee, 1972; Member: Section of Corporation, Banking, and Business Law, State Bar of Texas. Member: State Bar of Texas; Arkansas and American Bar Association; American Counsel Association; Texas Association of Bank Counsel (President 1983–1984). Fellow: American College of Trust and Estate Counsel and Texas Bar Foundation.

## Walter P. Zivley, Houston

Born August 5, 1931, in Mineral Wells, Texas. Southern Methodist University (B.B.A. 1953, LL.B. 1955). Admitted to bar, 1955, Texas. Member: State Bar of Texas, American Bar and Houston Bar Associations. State Junior Bar of Texas (director, 1961–1964; chairman of board of directors, 1962–1963); Houston Bar Association (director, 1966–1968); Member: Committee of Section of Taxation, State Bar of Texas and Committee of Real Estate, Probate, and Trust Law Section, State Bar of Texas, chairman, 1975–1976; Committee of Tax Section of American Bar Association. Fellow: American College of Trust and Estate Counsel. Partner: Liddell, Sapp, Zivley, Hill, and La Boon, Houston.

## The Editor

## Charles A. Saunders, Houston

Born January 18, 1922 in Boulder, Colorado. University of Houston (B.A. 1942), University of Texas (LL.B. 1945), Fraternity: Phi Kappa Phi. Admitted to bar, 1945, Texas. Member: State Bar of Texas, American Bar and Houston Bar Associations. Chairman, Minimum Continuing Education Committee, State Bar of Texas, 1985–1989; Chairman, Real Estate, Probate and Trust Law Section, State Bar of Texas, 1966–1967; Editor, *Texas Estate Administration*, 1975; Director, Advanced Estate Planning and Probate Course, 1977; President, American College of Trust and Estate Counsel, 1978–1979; member, The International Academy of Estate and Trust Law; Listed in "The Best Lawyers in America"; Partner, Fulbright & Jaworski, Houston.

# Index

172